Praise for The Self-Employed Life

"Becoming self-employed is a dream for many. But without the right strategies in place, the reality can sometimes be confusing and frustrating. Jeffrey Shaw's new book provides a valuable resource that will guide any entrepreneur—new or experienced—to sustainable success."

DORIE CLARK, author of *Entrepreneurial You* and executive education faculty, Duke University's Fuqua School of Business

"Jeffrey Shaw shows you the critical link between your own growth and that of your business. This book is your guide to pulling off both."

MIKE MICHALOWICZ, author of *Fix This Next* and *Profit First*

"*The Self-Employed Life* gives business owners the integrated perspective and tools they need to not only build a powerful business model, but also to enjoy their lives while building it. A fun and accessible read that will help you awaken your creativity, change your habits, and strengthen your brand."

PAMELA SLIM, author of *Body of Work*

"While being self-employed has long been a dream for a lot of people, most have no clue where to begin. Jeffrey Shaw offers practical advice that's rooted in deep experience running his own businesses. *The Self-Employed Life* will provide you with the tactics and mindset you need to thrive as a small-business owner."

TODD HENRY, author of *The Motivation Code*

"Jeffrey Shaw has created the definitive guidebook to being successfully self-employed. You'll return to its wisdom time and time again—guaranteed."

LESLIE EHM, author of *Swagger*

"Welcome to your very own business mentor disguised as a book. Jeffrey Shaw asks you the questions you are often afraid to ask yourself. Let *The Self-Employed Life* be your best friend on the bumpy road of entrepreneurship."

PHIL M. JONES, self-employed since fourteen years of age and bestselling author of *Exactly What to Say*

"*The Self-Employed Life* is a breath of fresh air. Instead of offering up the same list of clichéd (not to mention exhausting) practices, Jeffrey Shaw's book provides a grounded, holistic, alternative approach to achieving sustainable success in the full spectrum of your life as a business owner. Through an approach that combines personal development, business strategies, and several powerful daily habits, *The Self-Employed Life* will help you become a bigger, bolder version of yourself—helping you to embody the whole reason you went into business in the first place."

DENISE JACOBS, author of *Banish Your Inner Critic*

"Jeffrey Shaw's approach to helping small-business owners take control of their lives and their businesses is inspired yet practical. Readers are provided with great takeaways, actions, and ideas they can implement right away. His three-pronged approach to success can help small-business owners reframe the way they think to create true and lasting change. This book provides a mindset shift that entrepreneurs truly need."

ANGELA KURKIAN, director of education, Professional Photographers of America

The
Self-Employed
Life

Business and Personal Development Strategies That Create Sustainable Success

Jeffrey Shaw

THE self employed life

PAGE TWO BOOKS

Cataloguing in publication information is available from Library and Archives Canada.
ISBN 978-1-77458-004-2 (paperback)
ISBN 978-1-77458-065-3 (ebook)

Page Two
pagetwo.com

Edited by Amanda Lewis
Copyedited by Steph VanderMeulen
Proofread by Alison Strobel
Cover design by Peter Cocking
Interior design and illustrations by Nayeli Jimenez
Printed and bound in Canada by Friesens
Distributed in Canada by Raincoast Books
Distributed in the US and internationally by Publishers Group West,
a division of Ingram

21 22 23 24 25   5 4 3 2 1

jeffreyshaw.com
theselfemployedlife.me

This book is dedicated to my mother, Marge Shaw, who may be the most natural marketer and self-employed business owner there ever was. The owner of a hair salon for some forty years, she had the most loyal clientele. Many customers came to her salon week after week for decades, and eventually brought their children. She effortlessly built forever relationships with her customers. She maintained friendships for sixty years with her girlfriends from high school who were in her wedding party, and stayed in touch with the friends, ex-girlfriends, and ex-wives of her three sons. To know my mother is to love her forever, and that is the best attribute any self-employed business owner can have.

She faced many challenges in her personal life all while maintaining her business. Through it all, she showed the strength, resilience, and grit that are characteristic of any successful self-employed business owner. She represents the self-employed life if ever there was one. Thank you, Mom.

Love,
Your youngest

Contents

Introduction

Being Self-Employed

'VE ASKED countless self-employed business owners why they went into business for themselves and they've all said the same thing: "I wanted to control my destiny." My reply has always been: "How'd that work out for you?"

I'll bet you know how that worked out. The great paradox—or myth, lie, conflict, or whatever you want to call it—about self-employment is that we are going to gain control over our destiny, but we are entering into completely uncontrollable circumstances. Anything from a change in market demand to a crash of the economy, advancement in technology, or a global pandemic can derail our carefully thought-out plan. Or, if we're fortunate enough to create a business that takes off and explodes into something bigger than we anticipated, the hours we thought we could control are suddenly out of our control as we struggle to keep up with demand.

The very likely scenario is that you are overwhelmed by the number of things to do for your business, trying to keep up with your personal life, perhaps taking care of other people, running in a million directions (or so it seems), and no matter how much your business is making, it all feels nothing like control. How do I know this? Because we've all been there. We have a lot on

1

the line, and it often feels as if we're clothes on a line being tossed and turned by every gust of wind or change of direction. How are we supposed to gain control of our lives when there are so many outside circumstances knocking us around?

Add to all this that we end up feeling like we're the odd ones out in the business world. Many business practices don't seem right for us, or feel pushy and creepy. We wonder if we should trust our own instincts or do what has proven to work for others. We spend a lot of time getting better at what we do and improving our skill set, but we may not love the business side, even though we know we need to deal with it. On one hand, we feel we need more strategies: marketing, sales, SEO. On the other hand, we know that we are often in our own way and then seek to develop personally. Sometimes it can feel as if we're working really hard but hardly getting ahead. We're running on a hamster wheel; we're a hot mess; we're all over the place. Pick your phrase. We think we're alone, but of course we're not, because countless other self-employed business owners feel the same way.

Then we're told—and I love this one—"It's not personal, it's business." When you're self-employed, it *is* personal. Every single bit of it is personal. You pour your heart and soul into your business. How could it not be personal? As much as I love the book *The Four Agreements* by Don Miguel Ruiz and understand the intent, I have to admit that one of the four agreements, that you don't take anything personally, has always gotten under my skin because it's very difficult to not take things personally when you're self-employed.

It's very possible you feel fragmented, almost as if being pulled in so many directions has broken you into pieces. No matter how hard we try to compartmentalize things, it's all integrated when you're self-employed. What goes on at home affects work and what goes on at work affects home. We are challenged every day and, yes, we take it personally.

That's why in this book I'm introducing you to the Self-Employed Ecosystem—it's the holistic approach to business that you need, integrating personal development with business strategies, the inner work with the outer work, the receiving with the action.

In a healthy ecosystem, one that thrives and is successful, all parts of the ecosystem are working together. If one element is off, it can derail the effectiveness of the whole system.

The Self-Employed Ecosystem is about creating the most effective environment for your success. In life and business, the best you can do is set up the perfect circumstances for what you want, then let it all happen. It's a blend between controlling and allowing. Success is certainly not built entirely on manifestation and wishing upon a star, but neither is it built entirely on hard work and pushing.

As it turns out, creating the environment and setting up the circumstances for what you want to happen is one of the greatest lessons learned over my career. In my book *LINGO*, I taught how to create the environment to attract your ideal customers. In this book, you'll learn how to create the environment through the Self-Employed Ecosystem to build the business and life you want.

Without even realizing it, I learned the power of "setting up the circumstances" early on, when I was starting out as a portrait photographer. I was driving past beautiful homes with perfectly manicured lawns and Belgian block–lined driveways, thinking about the long shot I was about to take. I had just entered the grounds of the Westchester Country Club, one of the most exclusive golf courses in the country, home of many PGA tournaments and esteemed past members such as business tycoon Howard Hughes and TV personality Johnny Carson. I walked up to the pillared facade of the massive clubhouse wearing a sport coat with the tags carefully tucked in so I could return it after what might turn out to be a rejection in all of two minutes. In I went anyway, with portrait photographs mounted on canvas rolled up inside a black tube, as well as some business cards, and sweaty palms. I was greeted immediately by a receptionist, and I asked if I could speak to the club manager. Without asking any questions, she summoned the manager to the front. Honestly, I had expected my visit to the club to end right there.

Out walked a pleasant-looking middle-aged gentleman, but still, being in my early twenties, I was intimidated. I introduced myself as an on-location portrait photographer serving a clientele similar to his own, and asked if I could simply show him some of my photographs. I pulled the rolled canvas portraits from the tube and made it clear I was just introducing myself, without any expectations or "ask." It was clear he was just being polite and was not happy with me taking up his valuable time.

At the end of my presentation, I reiterated that I just wanted him to know I existed should any of his members ask about the services of a portrait photographer. With a forced smile, he shook my hand and said, "I doubt that will be the case, but thank you."

Two days later my phone rang, and it was the manager from the golf club! He said, "In the fifteen years I've been here as a manager, no one has ever asked me about a photographer. One of our members just stopped into my office to ask if by chance I knew a family photographer for a reunion they were hosting at the club. Whatever you're up to, young man, you're onto something." I did the family portrait session at that reunion, as well as countless other portraits at the club and for the members of this exclusive community.

Things like this in business don't happen by chance. Nor are they forced. The magic is in setting up the circumstances for what you want to happen. With the well-rounded and complete Self-Employed Ecosystem this book offers, you'll learn how to set up the healthiest and most vibrant environment possible to create the business and life you desire. *The Self-Employed Life* helps you take your rightful place in the spotlight and proudly claim "self-employed" as a description of who you are.

Let's break that down even further. How do you describe yourself right now? Do you say that you're a small business? An entrepreneur? A solopreneur? Freelancer? Let's look at the differences and implications.

Small Business

Many of us are quick to call ourselves a small business. Nothing wrong with that, except the fact that a small business is usually defined as having fewer than five hundred employees. That doesn't come close to describing most of us self-employed business owners.

The bigger problem is that it's a clear case of where size does matter. I assure you, if you go into a bank seeking funding and considering yourself a small business when you're a business of one, you will not receive the same funding opportunities as a 250- or 500-employee business. You will likely be seen as someone monetizing a hobby. There have also been numerous times, such as during a crisis like the Great Recession, when financial aid for small businesses has required a minimum number of employees, perhaps ten or more. So, we can be too small to be considered a small business.

Entrepreneur

Probably the most common term we use to describe ourselves is "entrepreneur." For many years, it was my preferred term to describe myself. However, "entrepreneur" isn't really a business model—being an entrepreneur is more a state of mind and an attitude. We think and act like entrepreneurs, which are attractive traits. It's kind of cool, to be honest, which is why I think a lot of us use the term. It captures the essence of our bravery. However, entrepreneurship tends to describe us, but doesn't really help us define our business. Some people even think "entrepreneur" holds a negative connotation, associating the term with being aggressive and hustling.

Solopreneur

I personally have mixed feelings about referring to ourselves as solopreneurs. This is definitely a term for which I think the vibe is important. I get it: a solopreneur is a business of one. But then I'd rather you referred to yourself simply as a business of one. There's a difference between being a business of one and going it alone. To me, solopreneur implies that you're in it by yourself. I feel like it degrades the significance of who you are and the big, bold, brave steps you have taken to be self-employed. In using the term "solopreneur," I think you are downplaying who you are and what you and your business are capable of. You're playing it small, and that's not the way to big success.

Freelancer

I quite like the term "freelancer." I like the "free to do as I please" part. A freelancer tends to work on a per-project or per-hour basis. They may have one area of expertise or a broad spectrum of talents. Freelancers are an integral part of remote and virtual work. They enable businesses to operate by being able to find talent in specific fields worldwide. Perhaps a downside of the term is that sometimes we're not perceived as having a legitimate business. A busy freelancer can indeed have a very legitimate business, but I wonder: What's the benefit of saying, "I'm a freelance designer" over "I'm a self-employed designer"? I think the latter conveys a bit more stability and intention to build a business.

Self-Employed

Having considered these commonly used terms and not feeling any of them are quite right, we come to the one term that actually fits. "Self-employed" clearly states the business model and describes the experience. To be self-employed is what it sounds like—we employ ourselves, and perhaps others as well. This is worthy of respect. The ever-growing community of self-employed business owners are the brave souls who are willing to dig deep and learn more about themselves in order to be successful.

Being self-employed is your badge of honor. It describes your business model, your tenacity, your commitment. And more than any other term, it also describes your life. So, own it. Whenever the opportunity comes up, proudly say, "I am self-employed." This ownership is also going to be important moving forward when it comes to seeking fair representation in the world of business and government. By breaking away from the association with small business, we can be sure that we are seen and get assistance when it's necessary.

I wrote this book for the vast majority of self-employed business owners—those who have fewer than twenty employees, and likely fewer than five. In the United States, 89 percent of small businesses have fewer than twenty employees. Even that can seem like a lot of employees, as more than half of small businesses don't hire anyone. I have plenty of support in the form of virtual assistants and contract help. My podcast is run by a small team. But they are not employees, and I, like many others, work alone at home. (Well, alone with my faithful fur baby.)

This book is for you and respects *all* of your self-employed life—not just the business part, but also the personal part. It offers a go-to manual on everything you need to be successful as a self-employed business owner.

I wonder sometimes what took me so long to figure out who I care most about: self-employed business owners. I've been self-employed my whole life—never had a "real job" or traditional paycheck. But after thirty-five years especially, as a self-employed photographer, speaker, business coach, brand message consultant, podcast host, and author, figuring out what needed to be done and when, adapting to an ever-changing world, going through the ups and downs, including two prior crises, 9/11 and the Great Recession, it is obvious now.

And as countries around the world initiated economic stimulus plans to respond to the COVID-19 pandemic, my first thought was, *Great. Yet another time in history when self-employed business owners are going to be overlooked.* I mean, how many times in life or business have you felt overlooked? Or is it so often you don't even notice anymore?

As it turned out, for the first time in US history, specific language in what came to be known as the CARES Act included self-employed business owners. This was a very pleasant turn of events, but more importantly, as far as I was concerned, the door was cracked open and I was not going to let it ever close again. Self-employed business owners matter. We matter to economies. We matter to communities. Of course, we matter to our families and ourselves. As a self-employed business owner—you matter.

In an interview on my podcast, *The Self-Employed Life* (formally *Creative Warriors*), Keith Hall, president and CEO of the National Association for the Self-Employed, pointed out that during times of job loss and layoffs, self-employment increases. Makes sense, right? People create their own jobs! I just had never thought about it until Keith mentioned it. Starting a business during such a challenging time demonstrates courage, grit, and integrity. To me, it shows a true sense of personal accountability and perseverance. That's hard-core.

In a video interview I did with Katie Vlietstra, vice president of government relations and public affairs for the National Association for the Self-Employed, she said, "I think this is a moment for the self-employed." She went on to say, "Up until the CARES Act, there really hasn't been fair representation for the self-employed. The sheer volume of self-employed businesses today is power." She emphasized that while it is a noble act to be self-employed, pay your mortgage, and perhaps employ a few people, the self-employed life also includes involvement in our communities, raising children, coaching soccer teams, and volunteering.

This is our time to come together as a community of self-employed business owners and take our rightful place in the spotlight. This is our time to be accepted in the business world and respected for our tenacity, sacrifices, and impact. We underestimate the impact we have on national economies and the role we play in creating change. When I asked Katie what she felt was the most important mindset shift she'd like to see among self-employed business owners, she said, "Step into your power. You have to exude that power. You have to understand the important role you play in the economy, the important role you play in the ecosystem of where you live and work."

So, clearly, now is also the perfect time for me to share this book. Perhaps you were trying to gain control over your destiny when you started your business, but it doesn't feel like it's quite working out as planned. That's OK. It's not entirely your fault. Until now, perhaps no one has really provided an alternative. This book presents the alternative you need—the Self-Employed Ecosystem. It is a proven method to help you gain as much control over your business and destiny as possible, and a guide to managing what you can't control so that you can stay on track.

If you've had moments of doubt, discouragement, and delusion, you're not alone. There's also a really good chance you wouldn't have it any other way. For all its challenges, we love the self-employed life.

1

Why We Work for Ourselves

T FOURTEEN years old, I could barely see over the steering wheel as my foot stretched out to reach the gas pedal. It was a Saturday morning and I was about to head out to do my weekly routine in my mother's Oldsmobile Cutlass Supreme, nicknamed the "Green Monster." I was a couple of years shy of having a driver's license, but considering it was a small country town, it wasn't likely I would get in trouble.

As always, I had butterflies in my stomach. I was stepping outside of my comfort zone. As I did every Saturday.

I was heading out to sell eggs door-to-door. Yes, chicken eggs. I had struck a deal with a local farmer to buy his eggs for twenty-five cents a dozen. He arranged to get the cardboard cartons for me. Every Thursday, my mother would drive me to the farm and patiently wait as I filled dozens of egg cartons. I had a very important strategy. Some of the eggs would have chicken poop on them, so I would clean most of them, but in every dozen, I left an egg or two with remnants of chicken poop on them. Why? Because it made them authentic. Just enough to be a little gross but let my customers know these were *authentic* fresh-from-the-farm eggs.

Now, the strange thing about where I grew up was that it was also the home of IBM's production plant, which was the largest computer production facility in the world at the time. My father was one of the first ninety employees at what was basically a blue-collar factory for high-tech computers. My mother, father, two older brothers, and I lived in a simple three-bedroom ranch home with one bathroom.

My father would talk about how someday there would be no need for cash and all products would have these barcodes on them to be scanned in the grocery store. I'd think, *Right, Dad.* Occasionally, my father would bring home the most recent computers, and I learned DOS at an early age. Then I'd get in the car and sell eggs. It was a weird juxtaposition between the latest in technology and the simplicity of country life.

Before I set out to cruise in the Green Monster, I had already packed up cases containing dozens of eggs for my mother to bring to her hair salon to sell to her customers. My mother's hair salon was a scene straight out of the movie *Steel Magnolias.* Blue-haired ladies would come in for their weekly wash and set and talk about life, their families, and likely a fair amount of gossip. Many of her customers remember the day I was born. My mother had probably one of the highest repeat customer rates of any business that ever existed! The same weekly customers for decades because going to my mother's shop was an experience and all about the relationship. As my family traveled the United States by way of camping (because that's all my parents could afford), if my mother saw something that reminded her of a customer, she'd buy it for them. It was a genuine, loving relationship between business owner and customer.

I charged $1.25 for a dozen eggs. Since I paid twenty-five cents wholesale to the farmer, my profit was a dollar a dozen.

Now, the going rate for a dozen eggs in 1978 was seventy-nine cents. I knew my price was higher than the market, but this was an intentional strategy. The first thing I learned in business is that pricing is arbitrary. You can charge whatever you want for anything. Regardless of what you charge, it's up to you to point out where the value is greater than the cost to your customer. Almost all objections to price in business is just that you haven't helped your customer see how the value or benefit to them is greater than the cost. Understanding that at an early age has been everything to me, and is no doubt how, years later, I was able to build a business as a high-end portrait photographer for affluent families.

What was the unique value proposition of my door-to-door egg business that justified the price? Partly, it was door-to-door service. We know service sells, right? But that wasn't the biggest factor. The biggest justifier of my higher price came from paying close attention to the customers I was serving. Because of IBM, employees were brought in from all over. Many were New York City transplants. And they, especially the stay-at-home moms, were in culture shock.

What could be cooler to city people than local, farm-fresh eggs? You could say I was selling cage-free, farm-fresh eggs before it was a trend. I even had one customer, our next-door neighbor, who was having a hard time adjusting to small-town living and would go back to NYC every weekend. She would buy dozens of my eggs and bring them into the city. I'm pretty sure she was marking them up even higher, but hey, that was her choice.

What I didn't realize at the time was that my simple egg business at fourteen years old would be the beginning of a lifetime of being self-employed. Remember when I said I had butterflies in my stomach heading out on Saturday mornings? It's because I was scared to death! I suffered from terrible shyness as a kid. I would take profits from my egg business and buy self-help

What motivates
us most is the
desire to become
**bolder versions
of ourselves**.

———————————

books by Wayne Dyer and hide them in my house because my family would think I was weird if they knew.

At one point, I even bought a book on self-hypnosis to hypnotize myself out of shyness. I learned how to visualize myself in a power pose among a crowd of people. The first time I tried my power pose, it didn't go so well. I was hanging out with a few neighborhood kids, which was already really unusual for me because normally I was locked in a room somewhere reading about how I could think and grow rich. But on this day, I thought I'd try out my power pose. While it may have felt powerful to me, the expressions I received told me I looked more like a cross between Superman and RuPaul. One kid looked me up and down and said, "What the hell's wrong with you?" That was the end of my self-hypnosis techniques.

So, going house to house and knocking on doors was a huge stretch for me. It wasn't just out of my comfort zone because I felt shy; the truth was, I didn't have a comfort zone at all. I felt out of place in the world. Knocking on these doors made me want to throw up.

Why do it, then? Sure, the money was motivating, but only to a degree—not enough to justify how scary it was for me. I actually chose photography as a hobby and later my career because it enabled me to withdraw. Back in the day, the darkroom at my high school was the ideal place to hide. I was a complete darkroom rat and was able to convince a guidance counselor to give me a permanent pass to miss gym class because it scared me so much. As I sought out things to photograph in the world, the camera became something I could hide behind. The irony was, I excelled at photography, which later put me center stage after I won numerous awards in high school. Then I was chosen by my classmates in photography school to be the student representative speaker at graduation. Talk about being so nervous you want to throw up!

Again, why do it, then? Why do any of this? What was so beneficial about selling eggs that I would put myself through all that? Why do any of us put ourselves through what we do as self-employed business owners? We know it's not the easy way. It may not be as challenging for most self-employed people as it was for me, but I do know almost all of us at some point think, *Why the hell am I doing this?* Have you ever really asked yourself that question? Is it really for the money? Is it really for freedom? Or control of your future?

There can be many reasons, but I believe the biggest reason we set out into the world as self-employed business owners is our desire to grow.

I believe that, whether or not we realize it in the beginning, what motivates us most is the desire to become bolder versions of ourselves—that is, developing into the best version of ourselves is bigger than any fear, challenge, or obstacle that we might face. It is even more important than the rewards of the business. With all our desire to make money, earn a living, and impact the world, we are first drawn, whether we realize it or not, to our own personal development. And that's why your personal development, combined with smart business strategies and supported by effective habits, is the key to your success.

Selling eggs door-to-door got me hooked on business, on the constantly dangling carrot to become more and do more. To find more in myself. I was fascinated by the way business worked and how it's like putting together pieces of a puzzle. From the outside, I was a seemingly shy, withdrawn, "probably not going to amount to much" kid. But on the inside, I was focused, determined, and curious about what I was really capable of.

Aren't you curious about who you can really become? How successful you can really be? What you are really capable of? I'll bet you are. Even just for a moment, let's put aside all the humbleness we've been led to believe we should have. Deep down, don't you already know there's greatness in you? I did. Even as that shy kid in a country town striking a ridiculous power pose, trying to dig myself out of the hole of fear, I knew greatness was in me and I was going to find it. No matter how long it took. No matter what I had to do. And in the spirit of most self-employed people, I'm still looking for it, because as much as I can see what I've accomplished and who I've become, I know there's more in me. It's why I stretch myself. It's why I take the risk of criticism to put my thoughts out there in the form of books that I believe can change people's lives. If not for the genuine desire to make a difference, I might shy away from taking the risk to change your life and business based on real-life experience and observation and not just education and degrees. We are self-employed because we want the room to grow ourselves and others, to do things differently, to help people as only we can. Because we don't know any other way. It's who we are.

Success State of Mind

Even today, when I get discouraged, the one thing that always picks me up is reminding myself that I have made every single dollar that has passed through my fingers. Every now and then I fantasize about having a "real job." My son always reminds me, "Dad, you're completely unemployable." He's not wrong. I don't know how I'd go from a lifetime of self-employment to working for someone else. I suspect I'd be a nightmare—never patient enough for committee decisions and never comfortable with fitting in a mold.

Like all business owners, I've been knocked down more times than I can count, have made stupid-ass decisions, and have recovered. I've learned that I've got this. You've got this too. With this book in your hands, we're in this together. You can email me, join the community Facebook page, or connect on other social media.

In the self-employed life, there is no division between personal life and business. Thus, *The Self-Employed Life* offers a holistic approach to business. Often, bringing together what appear to be opposites makes us whole. I like to describe the ideal state of mind as a business owner who is highly energized and calm at the same time. It's the way to move forward yet be clear of mind. It's not an easy state of mind in the ever-changing world of self-employment! Incidentally, aquamarine, the color chosen for the cover of this book, represents exhilaration and calmness, which is the perfect state of mind for success. Aquamarine can also be the color of the ocean, where the waves can be seen as tumultuous or soothing. In our self-employed lives, we want to have the energy to take the world by storm and to do so in a clear-headed, calm manner in order to make the best decisions. #BeAquamarine!

As we move through the Self-Employed Ecosystem, there may be chapters that you feel inclined to skip, thinking they aren't for you. Please don't. What I'm offering is a different approach to business, a complete system with many parts. It's the sum of all the parts that makes the system work. If you work only on specific parts, you'll stay stuck in the same loop or not become all that you are capable of being. If it feels a little woo-woo at times, hang in there because here's the deal: my woo-woo has a practical application with tangible results. If my woo-woo is going to make my business grow and yours too, I'm more than fine with that. Woo-woo all the way to the bank. Or, as I like to say on social media, #woowooinyourwallet.

Being self-employed is a unique experience, underserved by business and self-help books. When I checked to see what

In our self-employed lives, we want to have the energy to take the world by storm and to do so **in a clear-headed, calm manner**.

---

books were out there for the self-employed, the majority were about taxes and "how to make six figures when you're self-employed," neither of which felt like they understood the whole picture of the self-employed life, the feeling of being pulled in many directions, and the strategies that work for our business size. That there were books on how to start a business but none on what to do once you're in business showed how alone we can feel. We just go about our business, figuring it out on our own. To fill in the gaps, we hire coaches to get our mindset right, and take courses on strategy and marketing. Is it any wonder we feel like we're wearing a thousand hats, running all over the place to get everything we need?

Now you'll have everything you need in one place because you'll learn the ecosystem of the self-employed life. Think of this book as a constant resource, one you keep handy and return to all the time. It's so jam-packed with strategies, you can't possibly apply all the actions at once. There are also thought-provoking exercises that will create major mindset shifts for you. And if you want to complete the exercises online or in a separate worksheet, I've got you—I created a download-able workbook at theselfemployedlife.me.

I don't know about you, but I trust instinct and wisdom more than anything. That's street-smart, and that's what you'll find in this book. As a photographer, I have observed human behavior through my lens for more than thirty-five years. Wow, can you learn a lot! I've had a podcast for more than six years, with more than six hundred episodes and over 1.4 million downloads at the time of this writing, which has provided immeasurable lessons from authors, leaders, and business owners. I've received more than one thousand hours of training as a coach and leader. The business and personal development strategies you'll be learning are the real thing—not out of a textbook or the result of a degree. They are time-tested, proven, and based on a constant need to figure things out, which is what we do as self-employed business owners.

I'm a big believer in reverse engineering. We get what we want out of life and business when we know what we want first, create the environment to make that happen, and apply the necessary action. Here's where I want you, my dear reader and business warrior, to end up after learning the Self-Employed Ecosystem: you are your best self, you are proud, you have a business you love that's rewarding you very well, and you keep changing the world.

So, buckle up. Let's do this!

2

The Self-Employed Ecosystem

YOU SHOULD be beyond proud of yourself for being self-employed. You contribute to your nation's economy. You may be raising a family or contributing to your community. You may be coaching soccer or Little League or volunteering for a cause. You are building relationships with customers and making an impact. Don't take for granted how truly remarkable it is that you are running a self-employed business while running your life. Again, though, you do not have to do this alone, or without guidance. That's why I've created what I'm about to share with you: the Self-Employed Ecosystem.

You are about to learn that you can have far more control over your business than you may have thought. You are also going to learn how to manage what seems to be out of your control, so you don't get derailed. You'll learn how to create sustainable success to even out the ups and downs that are inherent in being self-employed, and you'll have everything you need in one place: personal development strategies that prepare you for greater success and bring out your best; business strategies that actually work for *you* as a self-employed business owner; and effective and efficient daily habits that create sustainable success.

This trifecta of personal development, business strategies, and daily habits is the formula for success—the Self-Employed Ecosystem. Why an ecosystem? Because an ecosystem is multiple interconnected elements where the whole works better than its parts. That's precisely what you need and how it works when you are self-employed. You don't have the luxury of checking out when you go home. You don't have a chance to not take it personally. You don't have a huge budget to hire people to solve problems for you. The self-employed life is running your business and your life, all mixed together all the time. Your personal development, the actions you take, and the habits you maintain, all integrated, all intertwined.

If one part of the ecosystem is off, it can destroy the whole. Look at what's happened to the Great Barrier Reef, the world's largest coral reef system, off the coast of Queensland, Australia. Composed of more than 2,900 individual reefs and 900 islands stretching for over 1,400 miles over an area of 133,000 square miles, *half* of the Great Barrier Reef has died since 2016 because of climate change. The water is too warm. One part of the system is off. As a result, the unnaturally warm ocean water destroys a reef's colorful algae, leaving the coral to starve.

Similarly, when one or more parts of your ecosystem are off, the entire ecosystem, your business or your personal life, can suffer. Businesses and relationships can die off. I guarantee you are working much harder than you need to in order to make your business and life work, without realizing it's because something is off, or out of order, in the ecosystem.

Maybe you have all the systems in place and are applying all the right strategies, yet you're still not getting the results you want. Or you've hit a plateau and wonder why you can't get to the next level. That's because, in the well-known words of the inimitable motivational speaker and author Jim Rohn: "Your level of success will rarely exceed your level of personal development."

I live by this quote because nothing could be truer when you're self-employed. Jim is pointing out that the way to reach your next level of success is to grow personally first. That's why success being self-employed has to begin with self.

Having a successful life and business requires that we first learn who we are, then do what we have to do in order to have what we want. This aligns perfectly with what this book is about—how I believe you create the environment for business success: develop yourself, take action, sustain your success, have what you want. That's the Self-Employed Ecosystem. *Be. Do. Have.*

Writer, speaker, and founder of Wordtree Marissa Polselli learned about the Self-Employed Ecosystem in my three-month Small Business Consulting program. She wrote, "I saw the interconnection between my capacity to grow my business and my personal development more clearly than ever before. I stopped trying to make this journey something it's not so I could revel in what it actually is. And I felt freer to lean into what my heart had already been telling me all along—that for me, it is all personal, and that's OK. In fact, it can be better than OK. It can be magical."

Stop trying to brush off that it's personal, and let that be the magic of your success.

The Symptoms of an Unhealthy Ecosystem

For an ecosystem to be healthy, all areas need to be working in sync. When they don't, there are symptoms of a problem. To understand your starting point, consider each of these symptoms to determine what part of your system is healthy and what part needs some work . . . or life support.

Symptom: You're working really hard but hardly getting ahead.

Cause: You are likely applying a lot of action, putting in a lot of effort, and always gaining new business strategies. You are constantly learning and growing. That's all great and important stuff! The problem is, you may be off-balance on the personal development side. You haven't prepared yourself to receive all the effort you're putting in. You probably feel like you're running on a treadmill because you're putting out a lot of effort but you haven't broken through the limitations of your own capacity.

Symptom: You've done a lot of personal growth work and found your purpose. You are clear on your mission and feeling ready. Sort of. You might think you're not really ready yet. Or that it's not perfect yet. You feel you need to continue to do more research and gain more information.

Cause: You've likely done a lot of personal development but aren't taking enough action. Maybe it's that you don't have the strategies and systems in place. It's a little bit of the "build it and they will come" mindset. You likely need to take more action to get things moving.

Symptom: You feel like you're caught in a loop. You create success but it doesn't last. You might even identify as self-sabotaging. You might feel like you take three steps forward and two steps back. Or two steps forward and three steps back. Success is sweet while it's there, but it feels fleeting. Or you feel stuck on a plateau.

Cause: You've likely done a fair amount of personal development. You're certainly putting in a lot of effort. In this case, there are areas of personal development that you haven't broken through that are holding you back. All the effort you're putting in is overwhelming you and keeping you from a more efficient way of running your business. And you haven't developed effective habits of sustainability, so the success you gain keeps slipping away.

I'm going to relieve you of some of the responsibility here. It's one of the inherent problems of being self-employed. It really isn't your fault. We have had to get all we need from too many different sources. But not anymore. With the Self-Employed Ecosystem, you have a chance to gain the control you seek all in one place.

Why the Self-Employed Ecosystem Works

I get it: You want results. Life and business success is both an art and a science. It's wonderful to create and build. That's the art side. But in order to get real results, there's also a science side: you need to test and measure. So, here's a little science so you can trust that the effort you're going to put in will lead to tangible results.

Several years ago, I was driving down the winding country roads of Connecticut in a recently purchased Land Rover with my three kids. One of my daughters, maybe about twelve years old at the time, said, "Daddy, before you bought this Land Rover, I'd never heard of it. And now it seems like every other car I see is a Land Rover." Since it was Connecticut, it was probably true! But think about it. Did all these people suddenly buy a Land Rover at the same time? Of course not. The truth is, they

The trifecta of personal development, business strategies, and daily habits **is the formula for success**.

---

were there all along. The difference was my daughter now knew what a Land Rover was and in turn couldn't help but see them everywhere. In social psychology, this is referred to as priming. We can prime our brains to recognize what we want to see. By "knowing" what a Land Rover is, my twelve-year-old daughter was primed to recognize Land Rovers and couldn't help but see more of them. In the simplest terms, you are far more likely to recognize what you already know.

How does the idea of priming support the Self-Employed Ecosystem? By having a system of the outcome you seek, you are far more likely to see it come true and recognize the achievements along the way. By doing the personal development work to unblock what's in your way, you open up opportunities that will prepare you for success. Having effective strategies and action steps for your business that really work will make your success inevitable. By having the habits that support you every day so you stay on track, you are far more likely to see the result of your efforts. By working through all the necessary components of success as a self-employed business owner, you will be priming yourself to recognize the success you want, whatever success looks like for you. If you can see it, you can recognize it. If you create it, it can come to fruition. If you have the tools, you can see it happen. So, priming and the power of psychology is one way the ecosystem is going to work for you.

Remember how the core challenge we face is that we are trying to control uncontrollable circumstances to gain power over our destiny? The Self-Employed Ecosystem empowers you to gain control over what you can by creating the best environment possible to increase your chances of success. While you still won't have control over many things in the crazy life of self-employment, you will be able to control the environment you create, and thus have considerable control of the results you see.

You'll have the marketing and branding strategies that will attract your ideal customers. You'll develop a profitable business model that makes sense for you. You'll gain the support, systems, and strategies you need. You'll learn the personal development strategies to grow and the mindsets to be sure you're not getting in your own way. With action steps that you can control and setting the stage for some serendipity, you will gain as much power over your outcomes as you possibly can. The rest is up to belief in yourself and trust.

You will have an ecosystem, all in one place, working beautifully in harmony as a well-balanced, healthy ecosystem does. Not that you'll be doing everything yourself. But you'll have a business that is healthy enough that you can hire the support you need to create the life you want. Isn't that why you went into business for yourself in the first place?

Create the Environment

It may have been one of the best marketing ploys of all time—at least, that I've ever been persuaded by. I decided to leave the cold NYC winter and head to Miami for three months. You know, the snowbird thing. In the back of my mind, I thought it might be possible that I'd move there; I had fallen in love with the relaxed lifestyle while frequently visiting a spa in Miami Beach. Whenever I was in the area for a speaking gig, I would find my way there. (By "in the area," I mean anywhere within a several-hour drive, because I had fallen in love with it that much.) So, it wasn't a stretch that I would move there, but by no means was I giving up my NYC apartment yet. To test out the various options of where to live in the Miami area, I rented two Airbnbs.

As the three-month visit was coming to a close, I had yet to find a place to live that really grabbed my attention. Sure, the weather was great, but in my heart, I was still a New Yorker. Repeatedly, though, people suggested I check out this residential area in Miami Beach called South of Fifth (which meant it was the five blocks south of Fifth Street). Even though there were several recommendations, I ignored them, because the last place I thought I wanted to live was Miami Beach. Don't get me wrong, it's lovely and fun, but super-touristy and a whole lot of partying. Just not my scene.

This is a good time to clarify what many people don't understand about Miami: Miami Beach is an entirely different town from Miami. Coming from the north, I'd always thought Miami Beach was the beach area of Miami. Nope. Miami Beach is a different town with its own government. There's South Beach, which mostly tourists and international travelers are familiar with. There's also North Beach. Miami Beach is on the barrier island, whereas Miami is a city on the mainland.

Now, the idea of living in the tourist area of South Beach was not appealing to me. Or so I thought. Just two weeks before bailing on the idea of living in the sunshine state, I decided to visit South of Fifth—and it was love at first sight. I was immediately enamored by the stunning park at the very tip of the barrier island. Standing on top of the bluff, I felt like Rose in *Titanic*, standing at the bow of the ship with her arms open. Seagrass waved gently in the breeze and the beach was stunning. I imagined dinners at the restaurant that was perched on the edge of the water. Within two days, I found an apartment, signed a lease, and drove to the local car dealer to hand over the keys of my SUV and leave with a beach-ready Mini Cooper.

A month or so later, I had an appointment with my new accountant, which I needed now that I was in a new state with new tax laws. I mentioned to him that I was surprised by how expensive my rent was. While worth it in my eyes, it was still the same rent I was paying in NYC. Sure, it was a larger apartment and on the beach. But it wasn't a savings at all.

"You do know that area was designed to attract New Yorkers, don't you?" he said.

"What do you mean, 'designed to attract New Yorkers'?" I asked, somewhat alarmed.

"Didn't you notice the park is designed after Battery Park in NYC?"

It's true, I thought. Also, Battery Park was one of my favorite places to hang out in NYC.

"Didn't you notice there's a Smith & Wollensky in the middle of the park?"

The restaurant is an iconic NYC steakhouse. True again. I sat back in my chair. *Damn,* I thought. I had been duped by my own marketing strategy.

In *LINGO,* I refer to this as the power of familiarity to attract your ideal customers: that is, recreating what feels familiar to your ideal customers in order to make them feel as if they are in the right place. This place, South of Fifth, felt like home. So, I made it my home. Without even being fully aware of the draw.

What was going on there is one of the most important lessons to understand about business today: It's far less about marketing and more about creating the environment in which people can make their own choices. It's a complete directional change, from how we used to think about business to how we need to think about business today. Now, you need to create the environment for the results you want. The most tweeted and posted quote from my talks is: "It's not your job to convince anyone of your value. It is your job to find the people who already value what you do."

Your success will not come from trying to convince anyone of anything. I resisted all the times it was suggested that I check out the area called South of Fifth. But once I had visited, I sure did convince myself very quickly.

**Having a successful
life and business**
requires that we first
learn who we are,
then do what
we have to do in
order to have what
we want.

———————

What built successful businesses in the past was selling your value—convincing people to choose you. What will get you to where you want to go in business today is *empowering people to choose you*. It's the difference between pointing out your value and explaining what makes you different or better, and attracting what you want toward you. The developers of this South of Fifth neighborhood understood the market they were looking to reach—in this case, New Yorkers willing to pay high rent because we were already accustomed to the price point. And I can say this as a New Yorker: we're tough! If it smells like we're being sold with a glossy ad campaign, it's a turnoff. In fact, chances are, if a real estate agent had taken me there and started pointing out all the wonderful attributes, it would have put me on the defensive to prove them wrong. As consumers, we do that sort of thing!

But making the area feel familiar to me and the scores of other New Yorkers I met living there—that was irresistible to us. Prospective buyers and renters like me looking to get away from nasty winter weather would see themselves living here. That's exactly what I did.

But let's make something very clear. While I jokingly referred to all of this as being "duped by my own marketing strategy," I never actually felt duped, and neither will your customers. I appreciated being empowered to come to my own conclusion and make my own decision. I highly respect the developers' wherewithal to care enough to understand what feels like home to New Yorkers, then present what they have to offer and let the customer make their own choice.

In every aspect of business that I can think of, it is our role as business owners to empower potential customers to choose us. This can come only from understanding their lingo and having empathy and patience. Podcast guest and author David Priemer exemplifies this perfectly in his book, *Sell the Way You*

Buy, which has quickly become one of my favorite books about sales. The concept is so simple but true. You know as a consumer you hate to be sold to. You pull back the second it feels like someone is trying to convince you of something. You avoid any situation that's going to feel "salesy." Why on earth, then, would you try to sell your services any differently from how you like to buy? You like to be presented with options, educated, and empowered to make your own choice. When a business or brand does this, you feel like they "get" you.

I believe we'll see even more customer empowerment in businesses moving forward. We'll see things like allowing customers to self-design their optimal experience, because the ideal experience for one person is not the same for everyone. For years, there's been so much emphasis that experience sells. While that's true, is it really best that businesses and brands decide what experience everyone is going to enjoy? How can it be, when not everyone defines a great experience the same way? It is better to empower customers to design the experience they want.

Some customers appreciate high touch while others prefer a more minimal approach. Maybe Burger King had it right all along when they said, "Have it your way." The more we can get clear on our offer and present our value in a simple and concise manner and back off, the more we empower customers to make an emotionally driven choice on their own.

Why is this difficult? Why is it so imperative we understand that what got us here (convincing) won't get us where we want to go (empowerment)? This is where I see a lot of self-employed business owners get tangled up. Let's make the connection back to what it means to be self-employed. It means you have put your whole self into your business. It's personal. You likely already harbor all the best characteristics that are required to empower your customers—things like empathy, the ability to listen, passion, being purpose-driven, having a customer-centric attitude. Let's face it. In running your business, you are coming from the ideal place not only because you care deeply but also because your livelihood depends on it! I'm not a fan of the phrase "the customer is always right," because they aren't. The wrong customer can be a nightmare, and no business has to accept that. "The customer is always right" only to the degree that you need their business, which is why it's imperative you have a business where you are free to work only with your ideal customers. Because your business pays your bills, you are likely to go the extra mile or two and put your whole self into it. So, your inner guidance is spot-on in empowering your customers.

The problem is, we don't see many examples in the grand scheme of things, so we doubt ourselves. We haven't detached ourselves from the outdated marketing and sales strategies in which we see other businesses participate. In our hearts, we know we shouldn't be trying to convince anyone of anything, but the next thing we know, we're looking at our websites and realizing they're nothing more than online self-indulgent brag sessions. In the complimentary reviews of websites I offer (see lingoreview.com to apply), I often compare how I experience a website to a cocktail party. Imagine you walk into a cocktail party and begin to tell people all about yourself, what you do, and how great you are at it. And then, as if that's not enough, you hand them a contact form to fill out. That's exactly what 90 percent of websites feel like. Businesses and brands talking all about themselves and then providing a contact form. I've heard more than enough selling—why would I want more?

I truly believe that most self-employed people know better than that. I can literally hear and see their sense of shame when I point that out. "Salesy" is the last thing they want to be. It's not who they are at all. Why, then, do small businesses come across that way? Perhaps it's because no one has pointed it out to them. More than likely, it's because we are bombarded by these outdated business mindsets all the time.

But do we want change? Do we want to create a better world? Do we want to contribute to our communities and those we serve in a positive way? Do we want the benefit of doing business the "right" way to result in a successful and profitable business? You bet we do. I've never met a self-employed business owner who didn't.

Success is about creating an environment so perfect that a branding professional from New York doesn't even notice how compelled he is because his heart spoke so loudly about what he wanted.

Now it's time to create the environment for you that will bring the results you want for a successful business and happy life.

personal develop- ment

S WE begin learning about the Self-Employed Ecosystem, there are a couple of very important things of which to take note. The first is the order in which the three elements of the ecosystem are presented: Personal Development, then Business Strategies, then Daily Habits. By no means do these three elements always happen in our lives in a linear way. But we do need a way to grasp the information, and they do comprise a healthy ecosystem, one following the other, so I present it to you in an intentional order. Just know that in real life as a self-employed business owner, I understand that all of these things often are happening at the same time.

The personal development strategies provide the motivation to create lasting change, pose powerful questions to unblock what's in your way, and equip you with strategies to move forward.

The business strategies are all about getting into action. This section is loaded with actionable things you can do right away to bring in more business.

The daily habits are all about creating sustainable success, evening out the ups and downs, and creating consistent, inward flow. Ahh . . . that feels good.

Now, I know you might want to get right to the things that are going to make you money—the business strategies. But keep those symptoms of an unhealthy ecosystem in mind. If you jump right into action without the personal development strategies, you will likely find yourself working really hard but not getting ahead. This is because the personal development strategies are what create the capacity for the success you're going to create by getting into action. I will say it again: *Your level of success will rarely exceed your level of personal development.*

Then I want you to get into action with all of the business strategies you can handle. There's a lot to cover, but you can also go back time and again for years to come. Once you've increased your capacity for success with the personal development strategies and gotten into action with the business strategies, then you need to learn the most effective and efficient daily habits I know of to create sustainable success. Once you have learned these strategies and habits in a linear way, they will forever be intertwined. An integrated ecosystem.

Throughout the following chapters, I'm very careful to focus on personal development and not self-help. Not that there's anything wrong with self-help as a category. I just want you to know that I don't in any way see you as someone needing help. I simply see all of us as capable of being more. I want to encourage you to leverage the best of who you are. To grow and expand and develop even further who you already are. That's why I look at it as personal *development*.

Believe me when I tell you that the key to increasing your business success is increasing your capacity to create success, receive that success, and manage it. In other words, there has to be a higher ceiling within you in order to reach a higher ceiling outside of yourself. I encourage you to do the work in these chapters. These are similar to the exercises I use with my coaching clients. You can do the work and answer the questions in each chapter, download the workbook at theselfemployedlife.me, or work on scrap paper or your phone. I don't really care how you do the work, just please do it.

Instead of just constantly taking action, ensure that your actions are going to pay off by confirming that they are going to work in the first place and then making sure the results are going to stick.

3

Get Out of Your Own Way

B EING SELF-EMPLOYED pushes more buttons and requires more personal growth than we can ever imagine. If you ask almost any success-minded person what they think is their biggest obstacle, many will say, "I am." We innately know there's something in ourselves that needs to be worked on, but if we take just one more online course or sign up for yet another webinar, or improve our social media strategy, maybe that will be the answer. With all the dangling carrots of just a little more effort, we keep thinking our big break is right around the corner, but in the end we are left wondering who the hell keeps moving the corner. This is because without developing ourselves personally, we don't actually get anywhere.

So often, people claim that they are their biggest obstacle. While there's some truth to that statement, it's not necessary to blame yourself. While I appreciate the personal accountability, that's not very productive.

The truth is, in most cases, no one has asked you the right questions to point out where you are getting in your own way.

In this chapter, you're going to look at some hard truths about what really motivates people to change and what are the right questions to ask ourselves to get out of our own way. Look at it as unblocking the path. These are the understandings you must have and the blocks that you need to get out of the way in order to move forward toward sustainable success.

Create Change That Lasts

What motivates people? I mean, really motivates them to make lasting change. Parents gamify dinnertime by making airplane noises to motivate their toddlers to eat vegetables. Or is it the threat of no dessert if they don't eat their broccoli? Is it the coach yelling from the sidelines who motivates you to move faster? Or the goal in sight that you're headed toward? Perhaps it's the promise of a bonus for a job well done. Or is it the threat of losing your job if you don't?

We frequently encounter this paradox of motivation in our lives. Without realizing it, we experience both sides of the coin, the push and the pull of motivation. We "push" motivation with the threat of a negative outcome (no dessert, yelling, or losing a job). We "pull" motivation with fun, goal setting, and incentives. But have you ever stopped to consider what actually works— pushing or pulling?

On one hand, it can be said that pushing generates more force than pulling. I think of the power of leaning in when you're pushing something. Perhaps a car that ran out of gas. On the other hand, there's supposedly less friction when you pull something. I think of how often I've chosen to drag something behind me rather than push it.

The bottom line is, from a physical perspective, I'm not entirely sure which is easier, pushing or pulling. I've looked it up and I always get opposing opinions. All I know is, it would never occur to me to pull a car that's out of gas. So, my mind says pushing is easier.

But let me share my viewpoint from the perspective of sea kayaking. My partner and I spend the majority of our weekends kayaking, usually for four hours every Saturday and Sunday, weather permitting. Along the journey, there are many times we get hit by a pretty rough current. Rob takes the back of the kayak; I take the front, only because years of yoga enable me to sit with my legs crossed and without a lot of back support, and he can't. In other words, he's got it easy! Except, he is the primary engine. Why? Because it's easier to push a kayak forward, especially when you're going with the current or directly against it. Just as in business, being in flow and going with the current is the ideal scenario. But there are plenty of struggles. Like being in a kayak when you're against the current, you are better off hitting those struggles head-on. The worst place to be is somewhere in between, battered from the side.

If Rob stops paddling, it's remarkably difficult for me, as the front guy, to gain any momentum, because I'm dragging all the weight behind me. Isn't that true of life? It's much more difficult to move forward when there's a lot of weight behind you. I'm going to teach you how the power of pushing away from what you don't want in order to move toward what you do want creates real change.

Let's look at motivation through another scenario. There was this church with a beautiful lawn, so beautiful that many dog owners would enjoy walking their dogs there. Unfortunately, not all dog owners are responsible, so there became an issue with lots of dog poop being left behind. In an effort to solve this problem, the church put up signs asking people to curb their dogs. That's a reasonable request, don't you think? But it didn't work. Those dog owners were still not picking up the poop. So, the church put up more signs. No change. They tried adding the threat of a fine. Apparently, that helped a little, but didn't come close to solving the problem. Clearly, the signs and even the threat of a fine were not enough to motivate these dog owners to change their habits. Finally, somebody had an idea, a different way to motivate the change. They placed a sign that read: "Children Play Here."

Guess what? The dog poop problem stopped. What created the change was inspiring people the right way. No one wanted children to have to play among dog poop. Understanding that children played on this beautiful lawn put it into context and gave it meaning. Certainly, anyone with kids would think, *I don't want my kids to play here if there's dog poop.* It didn't even take having kids to be motivated. In context, it just seemed gross. The problem went away.

We are often encouraged to make changes in our lives only through positive motivation of what we want to go toward. Pulling, you could say. Don't get me wrong: I love a good dose of positive motivation. But many people have become frustrated by the hype and promise of overt motivation that doesn't actually lead to tangible change. They end up thinking their stagnation is their fault.

I know you want tangible results. Still, wanting to go to the next level in your business or to get unstuck requires big, lasting change. Being self-employed is no joke: if your life and paying your bills are contingent on your business, you need real change and real results. So, we need a better way to motivate big change, at least as a jumping board. Think about it. How does a swimmer get started? By pushing off the edge of the pool.

The best way I know of to create lasting change is to get very clear about what it is you want to push away from. That's the jumping board. It's what gets you going and keeps you motivated to move forward. You actually have to grow to hate what you want to get away from in order to give it your all to move forward and never go back. I know that "hate" is a harsh word. But it can't be a "sort of dislike" or a "would kind of rather not have." Without the strong push, the change you want is just a "nice to have," and you're not likely to stick with it.

I'll offer a specific instance, which I have seen more than once with coaching clients. Money and finances are very touchy topics. In my book *LINGO*, I shared my own struggles with money when I was starting out as a photographer and didn't have even $150 to pay myself. I also mentioned that something I learned along the way was that money reveals truths, and the truth I discovered during the struggling years was that I was faking it until I made it, and it was painful. It kept me out of reality and away from owning the truth to do something about it. Until I was ready.

Money reveals the truth of how you present yourself to the world. How you spend money reveals what you prioritize. Isn't it funny how often you can come up with the money when you really want something? Money reveals your mindset. Are you scarcity-minded or abundance-minded? Money reveals your fears. Do you hold on to money tightly for fear of not having enough, or do you spend excessively for fear of the responsibility of having it? Money reveals where we are stuck.

These are hard questions that may stir up a lot of emotions. Let's tackle another hard truth about money. Whether you have a lot or a little does not define who you are; what you do with what you have may. If you're reading this book, I trust that you are the purpose-driven, soul-centered business owner I'm accustomed to meeting. Quite honestly, I don't worry too much about you becoming less likeable if your business is wildly successful, although many business owners seem to mind. Have you ever said or thought, "I don't want to become that person"? I hear that a lot! Who is it you're afraid of becoming by being successful and having money? A bad person? A shallow person? How likely is that, really?

What happens is that, too often, business owners become attached to not having enough. They fear turning into someone they wouldn't like if they were successful and had more. They're attached to the lessons they learn from not having enough, and are thus caught up in a cycle of scarcity. But then they say they don't like it and want to change. They take courses and read books about changing their circumstances, but nothing really happens. They hire a coach to change their business, which may work, but it may not change the financial cycle they are stuck in, so they still end up broke even if their sales improve.

This is all because, as I said earlier, it's not just the business that needs to change; it's the owner. One of my one-to-one coaching clients, Barbara, sought out my support to build a coaching practice. She was successful in her field and wanted to help others reach the level of success she became known for in her industry. However, her financial house was not in order. Now, let me say that I think it's unfair to uphold successful people to a higher standard of financial well-being. The truth is, we don't know the circumstances of someone's life. An expert in the field of finances can be going through a rough time financially due to personal circumstances or maybe a business deal gone wrong. Likewise, is it really fair to assume a marriage counselor has the perfect relationship? I agree there's a line of false image that crosses integrity. But we also shouldn't assume a professional can't be exceptional at helping others handle something they struggle with themselves. As they say, it's easier to do for others than it is to do for ourselves.

So I was fair to Barbara in that I understood her desire to help others in her field be successful, even though she was struggling financially. She even fell a few months behind on

**Getting clear about
what you want
to get away from**
sets you in a positive
direction, away
from what you
don't want in your
life anymore.

———————

paying for her coaching. She knew her struggle. What troubled me most, though, was how often she would view her struggle as a lesson that would allow her to better help others avoid the same situation. There seemed to be a bit of a martyr complex going on. While risky, I felt it was my job as her coach to bring it to her attention.

"You know, Barbara," I said, "for as long as you see a benefit of being broke and think it is somehow in service to others, you will continue to be broke." I know it was an eye-opening conversation, and hopefully it was a life-changing one. Unfortunately, I never found out because she couldn't pay for the rest of her coaching. This is one of the problems of not finding the real motivation to make the changes you want—the people around you who want to lend their support may lose their patience or capacity waiting for you to change.

As I shared before, the strongest motivation for change is to grow to hate what you want to get away from to the degree that you are willing to make the changes necessary, stick with them, and never go back. True in money, true in weight loss, true in leaving an abusive relationship, true in addiction.

The first chapter of the Self-Employed Ecosystem focuses on motivation and change because everything after is a moot point unless you are clear on what you want to get away from with such conviction that you will do something about it.

So now you have to ask yourself: What is it you want to get away from? I mean, *really* get away from—like, you hate it so much you don't ever want to go back there.

1. Is it not having enough money?
2. Is it working endless hours and feeling that life is passing you by?
3. Is it the feeling of being stuck?
4. Is it shame that you are not where you thought you'd be?

5. Is it accepting mediocrity in yourself when you damn well know you are capable of greatness?
6. Is it not being noticed?
7. Is it feeling invisible?
8. Is it feeling unvalued?
9. Is it being stuck in a job?

This is so important that I want you to stop and consider this question and fill in the blank: What is it that you are so tired of, that you have grown to hate, that you never want to face again? _____

Keep your answer short and clear. This is your monster in the woods that you want to leave behind once and for all.

Can you see how getting clear on what you truly want to change can motivate you? Can you see how not being sick and tired of it enough can cause you to stay stuck in a loop? You have to be truly done with whatever it is you hate. You have to detach from being OK with whatever it is in order to move forward.

With what you want to get away from being clear, now you want to remove any obstacles, mindsets, and ways you might get in your own way.

Get Clear About the Big Questions

Getting clear about what you want to get away from sets you in a positive direction, away from what you don't want in your life anymore. Intentions, when done in the From-To format, which you'll learn about in the next chapter, create a clear direction as to where you are going. As with any other journey, when you start in a new direction, it's possible you'll come across some obstacles in your way. If you go on a road trip, the obstacle may be traffic. If you set out on a hike in the woods, the obstacle may be a fallen tree obstructing your path. And when you embark on the journey of self-employment, the obstacle is likely going to be yourself.

Keep in mind that an ecosystem is a delicate integration of many components. When those components are working in harmony, the ecosystem is healthy and thriving. When even one part of an ecosystem is out of whack or not functioning well, it affects the health of the entire ecosystem. The blocks that you're going to explore and remove in this chapter are an important part of the health of your Self-Employed Ecosystem. If you don't get these obstacles out of the way, you may never have a truly healthy ecosystem working on your behalf.

I'll present these three obstacles, or mindsets, in the form of a question for each, and then you can provide your own answer. The goal in looking at these questions is to bring the blocks into the light. By doing so, they tend to lose their power. I've always loved the line from the Leonard Cohen song "Anthem" that goes, "There is a crack, a crack in everything / That's how the light gets in." We are not flawless. We're not striving to be. Asking yourself these important questions creates the crack. With awareness and shedding light on how these three mindsets may be holding you back, hopefully they will dim and lose their power so that you are free to move forward.

What negative mindset do you spend too much time in?
This question deliberately uses "in" rather than "on." To say it's a mindset you spend time *on* can imply that you are outside of the mindset, or that it's just something you are working on separate from yourself.

But in order to get to the root of the answer of what has you stuck, you have to be caught up in it, probably on a daily or very frequent basis. You have to consider how you are caught up in it to see how it could be preventing you from moving forward. Isn't that what's implied when we say we are caught up in something? That it's wrapped around us, trapped us, is holding us back? Think of it as a net that your foot is caught in.

So really, the question is: What negative mindset do you spend too much time being caught up in? Perhaps you can see now why you must get it out of the way in order to move on.

Perhaps your block is worrying. Do you spend so much time worrying that you're not productive? Do you worry about things that might happen and ruminate about things that did happen? Worry is a huge energy suck, and as you probably know on some level, almost all of what you worry about never comes to fruition. Do you lose sleep worrying about things in your business? Do you find yourself running a lot of "what ifs" through your mind?

How about "I'm not good enough" or "I'm not ready"? Is the vicious little voice in your head holding you back?

What about procrastination? Do you find yourself being less productive than you'd like to be because you tend to put things off? In my experience, people who procrastinate rarely put off identifying as a procrastinator but struggle to break the habit. A lot of time can be spent and lost procrastinating.

What about perfection? Is perfection really a negative mindset? Perhaps not always, but the consequences certainly can be. Is your drive for perfection possibly based in insecurity, or not being good enough? Or is the negative mindset the consequence of not being perfect?

What about feeling overwhelmed? That's my personal gem. I waste way too much time feeling like I can't handle it all, which can be paralyzing. If I keep quietly telling myself I can't handle it all, how can more of what I want come my way?

How about self-sabotage? That's a doozy. Do you get caught in the cycle one step forward, two steps back? And then do you waste even more energy beating yourself up about self-sabotaging?

When Christopher, a sixty-something former certified public accountant, began my Small Business Consulting program, his negative mindset was about not feeling relevant. He was so afraid of not being able to keep up with changes in technology, online marketing, and the latest in social media that his negative mindset metaphorically built a wall around him to keep him from moving forward. His real fear of technology made him feel irrelevant in today's business climate. Yet, he had a passion to serve others with all he knew about finances. I asked him one day if he was afraid he was going to break the Internet. Sure, he laughed, but it wasn't without merit. He came to realize that for as long as he felt disconnected in today's world, he was not going to be comfortable leveraging technology to build his business.

Then, of course, there's fear. Fear is a negative mindset that keeps us afraid of risk, even if we're minimally moving forward. But when our minds are creating all the worst-case scenarios, we aren't really present, which makes it difficult to advance toward any goal at all.

The point I'm making about these negative mindsets and the reason you must shed light on and change them is that you're wasting energy in these blocks that you can't afford to waste. Being successfully self-employed takes everything you've got. You knew this wasn't going to be the easy road to riches. You need every bit of energy that is available to you. To be full of enthusiasm, to be focused, to apply all your effort and keep on going.

While there are likely multiple negative mindsets that keep you from success, what's the big one? Which negative mindset really makes you feel stuck? What's the primary negative mindset that gets in your way and wastes your energy? We need to get that out of the way!

It takes discipline to keep your negative mindset at bay. But you can't fully move forward without clearing the path. Noticing when you are caught up in your habitual negative mindset and putting it aside is one task to get you moving in the direction you want to go.

Here are a couple of questions you can answer to get you started:

The negative mindset I spend too much time in and that is wasting my energy is:

_____

_____

You also need a way out of that negative mindset. Try this:

When these limiting thoughts and beliefs come up in the future, I'm going to say to myself:

_____

_____

This leads us nicely to the second question.

What belief do I have to let go of in order to move forward?
Imagine you're Tarzan in the forest, swinging from vine to vine. Tarzan always has to let go of one vine in order to grab the next. There's simply no other way to move on. There's always something you have to let go of in order to move on. It can be scary!

I was once at a rope course, like an obstacle course, and there was this crazy challenge to climb very high up in a tree. I had always had a fear of heights, so at this time, the climb up the tree was frightening. Granted, I was wearing a harness and there were two strong guys keeping me safe. But do you think my unreasonable mind full of fear of heights registered that I was held safe by a harness? Of course not! After a long climb up the tree, I arrived at the destination, a cable to walk across to another tree, seemingly miles away. (OK, not *miles*,

We don't let go of something until the benefits of what's ahead are greater than what we've been holding on to.

---

but it was far.) The cable was wobbly and swinging. Above it there was another cable, quite high up, from which several thick ropes hung all the way to the other tree. The ropes were there for people to hang on to and steady themselves as they began the journey to the other side. The problem was, each rope would run out of length no matter how much I spread my arms to reach the next rope. There was just no way to grab the next rope without letting go of the one I was leaving behind. I had only a moment between letting go of one rope and grabbing the next. Probably just a split second and one step, but it was scary letting go; it felt like a very long gap and a very long way down. But if I didn't do it, I would be stuck where I was.

At big stages of growth in our lives especially, there's almost always something to leave behind—a belief, a negative story we repeatedly tell about ourselves. These may have served us at one time, but now they make us stagnant. Letting go is the pattern breaker. But we don't let go of something until the benefits of what's ahead are greater than what we've been holding on to. In his book *The Iconist: The Art and Science of Standing Out*, Jamie Mustard talks about the irony of business owners who want to be seen, to be iconic, but who often hold themselves back from being bold enough in their brand messaging to achieve this because they're uncomfortable with the potential of being seen negatively. So long as you maintain the idea that being in the spotlight is self-centered or means you're full of yourself, or you are afraid of the responsibility of being in the spotlight, you're not going to step forward and take your rightful place there. You have to let go of the modesty nonsense in order to meet your desire.

Old beliefs become your self-fulfilling prophecy. Looking back on my personal life a while ago, I noticed that while I was in different relationships, I would always end up feeling the same way—that I wasn't getting back as much as I was giving. It took a therapist all of ten minutes to point out that I was giving so much in my relationships, way beyond what should be given, that it was practically impossible for someone to give back nearly as much. He pointed out, "You are literally setting up your relationships to fail." Boom!

In order to break the pattern and get the results I wanted (a loving relationship), I had to let go of the belief that I was never going to be treated as well as I treat others. I had to choose to either give with no expectation in return, or moderate how much I gave so I wasn't bending over backward, giving my all and revolving my life around the other person. Turns out, it took a little bit of both, although setting boundaries for how much to give made the biggest difference.

By now, you clearly understand that to move past your current state toward better, you need to check your negative mindset. Maybe it's a belief that no matter how hard you work, no one will notice. Or, that success is somehow going to change you into someone you won't like. Or that success is for everyone else. Perhaps you think you don't deserve the spotlight. Forget that crap! You simply have to identify it, call it out, and decide that you are done with that old belief. Otherwise, even if you move forward a bit, that nonsense is just going to keep pulling you back. Using this Self-Employed Ecosystem, we are definitely not looking to end up in the same place. You definitely are not looking to work so hard in your business year after year only to keep ending up in the same place.

Time to call out your obstacle:

What belief do I have to let go of in order to move forward?

_____

_____

_____

_____

Whereas the two previous questions were pretty specific, about a certain negative mindset and a belief you have to let go of, the following question is broader.

What *fundamental* mindset shift do you need to make?
There's likely a way you look at life that is so natural to you that you don't see how it's holding you back. That's the reason for considering what fundamental mindset shift you need to make in order to open up bigger opportunities and grow. It's likely a way you have trained yourself to think up to this point. It's keeping you small. In my case, literally small.

As a photographer, my business was based entirely on volume control. Whenever I got too busy, I'd raise my rates or restrict my calendar. From the day I became a professional photographer, I always knew I wanted a business based on quality, not volume, and that I never wanted to hire other photographers. I was going to create a high-end portrait photography business based on a personal brand.

For the peak years of my business, I did about 150 portrait sessions a year. Of those, over half were repeat clients—some annually, some every two to three years. But conservatively, seventy-five clients a year would be repeat business, which meant I had to gain only seventy-five new clients a year. Phew! That suited me just fine, not only from a marketing perspective, but also because I was perfectly happy not having to meet a lot of new people every year. At my core, I still consider myself a pretty shy person. You'll hear a similar dynamic from many introverted people: On one hand, they don't like the spotlight. On the other hand, they like the attention they are rarely given. Many introverted people are so used to handling uncomfortable situations, they become highly skilled at showing up in the world appearing to be a lot more comfortable than they really are. I believe this is why so many professional speakers identify as introverted.

All this is to say, I liked my limited number of clients. I liked my somewhat protected life, living on six acres in a lovely Connecticut town, raising a family. And I was comfortable with my small, very select group of friends.

Until I wanted more.

I grew to want to have a much bigger impact on the world. I stretched myself way outside of my comfort zone and stepped onstage as a speaker. While in a leadership program, I took on the challenge to start a podcast to see what would happen if I was the host. As a photographer and speaker, I thought of myself kind of like a professional guest. (As I like to say, I was the one who always had to ask where the bathroom was.) But this started making me question my value. My whole life, actually. Was I successful only because I "forced" myself on people? Was I actually better at marketing than I was talented as a photographer? Did people find me worth coming to, or was all my success based only on my hard work? Would anyone say yes to being my guest on the podcast? Would anyone show up to listen?

So, I started a podcast called *Creative Warriors* to find out. I stretched even more and tweeted at someone I greatly admired, asking if she'd be my first guest. Sally Hogshead said yes. For my second guest, explaining I didn't even have a following, I asked *New York Times*–bestselling author Michael Port. He said yes! My first month, fourteen hundred people showed up to listen. I had no idea if that was good or bad, but it sounded pretty good to me.

When I started the podcast, someone asked me what impact I hoped the show would make. I said, "It would be amazing to impact fifty thousand people a year." Coming from a mindset of limiting my clients to only 150 people a year as a photographer, fifty thousand people a year through the podcast was a mind-blowing concept. But the podcast, renamed *The*

Self-Employed Life, now reaches thirty thousand listeners a month or more and is growing.

The fundamental mindset shift I had to make was about small numbers: I had to stop seeing the world in small numbers in order to make a big impact.

When I met Cheryl Kaiser, we had been in photography for almost the same amount of time. She was looking to make changes in her photography business. Years later, she decided to become a coach and asked that I train her. She and her husband live in a lovely area in the northeast and had recently become empty nesters. Cheryl was clearly very comfortable and well known in her community. She showed interest in having a much bigger impact on the world as a coach and founder of The Moxie Sisterhood, which is an online community of women rediscovering their moxie after devoting their lives to raising a family.

I suggested to Cheryl what I thought her biggest challenge would be and the fundamental mindset shift she would have to make in order to go big: her local mindset. As a local photographer and being so involved in her community, as wonderful as that is, Cheryl would be unable to think big. She would have to start thinking global to step into all she was capable of being. Fortunately, Cheryl is one of the bravest people I know. It was important to her to shift her local way of thinking to thinking globally in order to create bigger world for her online community.

Another example of a fundamental mindset shift: a woman on a singing competition show came to understand that in order for her to become the star she wanted to be, she had to stop thinking of herself as the background singer she had always been.

Now it's your turn. In order to get a different result, you have to see the world differently. This way of thinking has served you well up until now, but now it's limiting you from going as big as you'd like.

What's the fundamental mindset shift I have to make to think bigger?

_____

_____

Having gotten out of our own way, now we can focus on moving forward.

4

What Moves
You Forward

WITH THE work you did in the previous chapter to get out of your own way and create a clear path, now you can move forward.

It's worth pointing out that getting out of your own way and moving forward doesn't have to be a long, drawn-out process. Have you ever heard something that completely changed your perspective almost immediately? It's what I refer to as a fundamental shift. When I outline my keynotes, I start with several fundamental shifts, and I intend on at least one sticking for each attendee.

Typically, if we can gain even one significant change in our way of thinking or in a business practice, we are more than pleased. It doesn't always take as much energy or as many hours on the therapist's couch to create significant change as we have been led to believe. There really is truth to the adage that life can turn on a dime.

The following two practices are the best I know in order to move you toward the success you seek: setting intentions in a way that really works, and holding your vision for your future in a more effective way.

Make Your Intentions Stick

I've always been a bit of an intentions junkie; I like exploring whether intentions work, and why, or what the difference is between an intention and a goal, an intention and prayer.

Lynne McTaggart's book *The Intention Experiment: Using Your Thoughts to Change Your Life and the World* was indeed life-changing for me. It was after reading it that I realized the true power of intention. To emphasize the possible effects of intention, Lynne shares the results of a research project done in Washington, DC, in 1993 to lower crime in the city. The hypothesis was that if enough people gathered and shared the same intention to lower the rate of crime in the city, the crime rate would actually be lowered. Between June 7 and July 30, 1993, four thousand participants in the Transcendental Meditation and TM-Sidhi programs by Maharishi Mahesh Yogi meditated on the intention of lowering crime. As a result, the maximum decrease in crime was 23.3 percent, which coincided with the peak number of participants meditating at the same time. So, the number of people meditating mattered. Even taking other nuances into consideration, the study showed a 15.6 percent reduction of violent crimes overall. Still very significant results. A time series analysis showed that the effect of the intention was cumulative and even persisted after the project ended. Also, calculation of the time series model predicted that a permanent group of four thousand coherence-creating experts in the district would have a long-term effect of reducing crimes by 48 percent. That means intentions "add up." Can you imagine that? If intention has the power to lower crime in a major city, how could it not have the power to change your life?

Envision what success means to you specifically.

———————————

When it seems that intentions aren't working for you, the problem is typically twofold: your method and your commitment. I'll address each.

Method: There are many suggestions for making intentions work. One is to get specific about what you intend. Many people are much too broad with their intentions. For example, it won't be effective to hold an intention simply to be successful. What success looks like is different for everybody. Therefore, it is often advised to get more specific on the outcome you desire—for example, a sales goal. You could have an intention to do $250,000 in sales this year.

It has also been suggested that you envision what success means to you specifically—what to you means you've arrived—say, a boat or a vacation home, and make that your intention. I get it, but it doesn't feel quite right to me. I'm not big on intending something material, even if it represents something bigger. It's tangible, yes, but it doesn't create a lasting shift.

To me, the intention of intention (meta, right?) is to create a shift. A dramatic and measurable shift. We want results. You are a busy self-employed business owner. You don't have time for nice-to-haves. You want real results in the most efficient way possible. You are in this for a significant change, otherwise you wouldn't have challenged yourself to get clear on what you want to get away from.

As we know, the next step after that is establishing where you want to go. The two are connected; one feeds the other. This is why I suggest making intentions with a very clear, simple format I call From-To, the most productive and efficient way to make intentions.

This intention format determines your starting and finishing points for your goal. For example: "I want to go from not having enough money [start] to having more than enough money [finish]." Note: I didn't say *to having enough* money. I said *to having more than enough* money. If the power of intention can lower crime in a city, can it not result in you having more than enough money? Don't sell yourself short.

Here's another example: "I want to go from being overlooked to being seen on the biggest stage as a speaker." You can even make it more personal by saying: "I want to go from feeling like I'm in the back of the line to taking my rightful place at the front of the line."

Answering one of my posts on social media, productivity expert Clare Kumar gave yet another example of a From-To intention: "I want to go from saying yes to too many projects to saying yes to only the projects that excite me!"

When Laurie Guest, a well-known and respected professional speaker, joined my Small Business Consulting program, I already thought of her as an icon in the speaking profession, an in-demand keynoter who commanded the stage. When we did this work together, I was surprised that the intention most important to her was to become better at completing things. From someone who seemed to have it all together! She said, "I knew instantly what I wanted to go from is my habit of not finishing things completely. I'm great at the ideas, planning, troubleshooting, and starting. No problem with that at all! However, the finishing is a different story. I've got piles of half-done projects, stacks of good intentions, and abandoned tasks everywhere. I'm sure somewhere in the house there is even a laundry basket at one stage of the 'clean clothes to be returned to the closet' project. This weakness of mine is annoying to those around me and a real albatross to my mindset."

In the From-To format, we sought a way to express Laurie's intention in clear and certain terms: she wanted to move from being a half-asser to a rock-star finisher. Once clear on what she wanted to move from, all Laurie had to focus on was becoming that rock-star finisher. Whenever the inclination came along to not finish something, she could say to herself, "Nope. Not today. I'm a rock-star finisher."

Within the week, Laurie had emailed me to let me know she was seeing evidence of the benefits of finishing her work projects, and that not only was all the laundry done, but it was also folded and put away.

To dramatically increase the likelihood of your intentions being productive and coming true, you want to understand your starting point and a specific outcome.

Time for you to state your intentions. You can have several, by the way, so go for it!

1. I want to go FROM _____ TO _____

2. I want to go FROM _____ TO _____

3. I want to go FROM _____ TO _____

4. I want to go FROM _____ TO _____

5. I want to go FROM _____ TO _____

6. I want to go FROM _____ TO _____

Now that you've gained a structure to make your intentions work, let's consider why they may not come to fruition.

Commitment: When intentions don't result in success, it's usually because of a lack of commitment. Again, imagine the level of commitment in the Washington, DC, research study to decrease crime. Four thousand people committed for just shy of two months. Since you likely don't have four thousand people to support your intention (could you imagine?), you will likely need more time for it to stick. I should add here that I like to look at intentions as *sticking*, not just working. Think about your intentions as having layers that are added day after day with your focus, like layers of adhesive.

Make your intentions stick by making them part of your daily routine, even a morning practice. I recite my intentions as I walk my dog in the morning. To the passersby, I nod and wave and maybe even say hello. But in my head, I'm reciting my intentions like a tape running in the background. Ultimately, you want your intentions to be so engrained, you just know they are there as you go about your day. That's why this From-To format of intention setting works. It's super-short and concise so you can really embody them.

Maybe you pause every now and then throughout the day and give your intentions some focused attention. Another tool is to use a trigger. Perhaps every time you hear a car horn, you recite your intention. I live not too far from Miami International Airport. When I'm going through a period of a more focused study of my intentions, which is usually early in the year, I use the sound of a plane flying overhead as a trigger to recite an intention.

With the From-To format of setting your intentions and your unwavering commitment to stick with them for the long haul, I am confident you will see the results of your intentions. But we're not done yet. We've barely begun building your Self-Employed Ecosystem. But isn't it getting harder already to imagine you won't be successful? By getting clear on what you want to get away from and now knowing how to set your intentions so they work to get you to where you want to go, isn't it seeming more likely the success you're seeking is inevitable?

There's a lot more to come. Next, let's get you clear on where you're going in a way that makes sense in today's world.

Make your intentions stick by making them part of your daily routine.

———————————

A Directional Vision

The final element of the Personal Development step of the Self-Employed Ecosystem is about you having a clear vision.

There are various tools for creating a vision and many people have formed a preference, whether it's meditation, journaling, or making a vision board. There's also more direct, detailed mental visualization, such as what a downhill skier might do before hitting the course. So, the lesson to have a clear vision of where you want to end up—the goal you have in mind—is not new.

The problem is that having *too clear* of a vision can lead to frustration and discouragement if you don't achieve it. I see this time and again among very goal-minded self-employed business owners. They have a distinct vision, set big goals, and are disappointed when they don't achieve everything they set out to accomplish. After that, maybe they decide not to bother setting other big goals or visualizing ideas: there's a cost to thinking big. So, what's a business owner to do? Have a clear vision of their growth objectives at the risk of disappointment, or set out to accomplish success without a good idea of where they want to end up? Or perhaps your vision comes true, but it looks different from what you expected.

All of this introduces the vision paradox. Is a vision really an expectation and therefore subject to possible disappointment? Is it possible to achieve a vision but not recognize it because it isn't exactly what you expected? But you have to have a vision of where you want to end up, don't you?

Years ago, I traveled to Ireland for a couple of weeks with my three kids. They were pretty young at the time—around fourteen, twelve, and nine. Old enough that it would be a memorable trip for them but also young enough that, as a single parent traveling with three kids, I wanted a reasonable amount of certainty in the planning. So, I turned to a travel agent to book and plan the trip. With two weeks available, we wanted to catch all the popular sites but not be too bound by a schedule. He found the perfect way for us to enjoy our time in Ireland, sort of a blend of vision without knowing exactly where we were going.

There was a program that enabled us to confirm a place for us to sleep every night without committing to exactly where. The program came with a very large guidebook with listings of all the participating accommodations. They ranged from penthouse apartments in Dublin to guest rooms in a farmhouse way out in the country to castles straight out of *Harry Potter*. Without committing to exactly where we'd land while traveling through Ireland in a rented car, we were guaranteed a reservation somewhere in the hundreds of participating accommodations. The added spontaneity enriched the experience. There were times we found ourselves in a fishing village that we loved and stayed longer than we'd planned. There was the time we got lost on a dirt road no wider than the car with stone walls on both sides. I truly have no idea what would have happened if we had come upon another car. But we were able to find a room in someone's home, and woke up the next morning to probably the biggest breakfast I've ever seen and a tour around an actual sheep farm. It was fantastic!

This idea of a destination with a loosely held plan, without having a concrete journey to get there, embodies exactly how I suggest we hold a vision. Directional but not definite. This seemingly open-ended version of a vision seems to suit self-employed business owners extremely well. Remember, the core frustration and internal conflict of being self-employed is that we go into business for ourselves wanting to control our destiny, then find ourselves in uncontrollable circumstances. Imagine, then, how potentially frustrating it can be to hold on to a vision too tightly only to realize the myriad things that can change that vision along the way. Inevitably, we're going to get lost down some backcountry roads. Maybe the view is even prettier. Maybe not. We can still get to our destination, but it may be better to hold a vision like an intention with a desired outcome rather than determining precisely the path to get there.

To further illustrate my point, here's another example of holding your clear vision in your sights while being open to the various possibilities of how to get there. I've already mentioned how much I love kayaking! As with a vision, when you're kayaking you lock your sights on where you want to go. Perhaps a beach in the far distance. Or a sandbar where fellow boaters are hanging out. Just a speck in the distance across the ocean at the onset of the journey. You quickly learn to read the current and flow. If you're paddling against the current, you learn to feel the force working against you as a way to propel you forward, the way a plane takes off into the wind to gain flight. You learn to position the bow of the boat to hit the waves at the right angle. If you don't, you're working so much harder than you have to when you keep getting hit from the side. You're far more likely to run out of steam if you're constantly working harder than you need to. You may need to meander a bit seemingly off-course, but the route is easier and far more efficient if you position yourself to work with the environment and not against it. In fact, as you hold your destination in sight, there's almost always an arc in the path to get there. Rarely do you get to your destination in a straight line. If you force yourself to, you are almost always guaranteed to be fighting with every stroke of the paddle. And there's always the possibility of an unexpected wave taking you out.

It always seems that when we have to go off-course on our kayak adventure in order to work with the current, we come across a family of manatees, occasionally even swimming under our boat. A dolphin is a wonderful treat. Like life itself, the greatest moments of joy always seem to be the unplanned excursions on the way to our destination. When these things happen, it feels like a reward for our willingness to dance with life.

In today's world of being self-employed, having a directional vision more than a definite plan is more important than ever. The world around us changes so rapidly. How could you possibly know how you're going to get anywhere? You have to be ready to pivot, maneuver, go with the current.

Vision is personal—there is no "one size fits all" method. Another effective method to reach the destination of your vision without knowing exactly how you're going to get there is to pay close attention to what you see every day. This way you are seeing your vision in small increments on a consistent basis instead of as something far off. My coaching client Tami expressed to me that she felt caught in a loop. She even described it as self-sabotage. Every time she reached a certain level of success in her business, she pulled herself back. As she said to me, her intention was to go "from survive to thrive." Thriving was her vision, and all of the things that in her view came along with a thriving life were carefully and artfully placed on a vision board. That's a wonderful vision! But even she stated that it seemed so far in the future.

I suggested that she begin to see her vision every day in every possible way around her—that she start noticing what is thriving around her: the trees, plants, overflowing stream, and so on. I told her about the banyan trees here in Miami. When their limbs grow, they drop a vine. When the vine hits the ground, it roots itself and turns into another trunk. So, as the tree grows and expands, it continually supports itself with another tree trunk. Brilliant, right? I can't look at a massive banyan tree without thinking about how it's thriving.

I challenged Tami to consider how she could see herself thriving right now too. Understandably, all she was feeling at that moment was that she was only surviving. She spoke about letting go of her car that was barely hanging on and requiring a lot of money to repair. I asked what would happen if she got rid of the car, which she stated she didn't really need, and used a ride-share service like Lyft or Uber instead. Instead of owning and driving a car that was barely surviving, how would it feel to arrive at her destination in the comfortable back seat of someone else's car? Wouldn't this feel like thriving and yet be saving a lot of money in repairs at the same time? Seeing your long-term vision in everyday life is a great reminder of where you're headed.

Having a directional vision without know exactly how you will accomplish it is more than keeping up in fast-changing times. It allows for you to grow. How can you possibly know what you're capable of three months from now if you're constantly growing? Wouldn't planning ahead actually be based on past information?

Conclusion: Personal Development

As we get into the practical business strategies, hold a big directional vision for yourself. There's a lot to come. You can't possibly know exactly how you're going to get there.

By doing the personal development work in this section, you have raised the ceiling of what you're capable of. I want you to appreciate the significance of the work you've done because this is what so many business owners overlook and what may have been missing in your own life. Often, we just keep applying action and it's almost like there's no more room for it to go anywhere. We end up feeling overwhelmed and not really getting anywhere. You've changed that now. You've done the inner work to prepare for the outer results. Let's look at all you've accomplished:

- You're clear on what you want to get away from and what motivates you to move forward.

- You're aware of the negative mindset that wants to creep in.

- You've let go of a belief that is no longer serving you so you can think bigger.

- You've set your intentions, being clear about what you're going from and what you're going to.

- You have a flexible and directional vision to see all that's possible.

You have increased your capacity for success and unblocked many mindsets that have been in your way. You have made your inner environment healthy and ready. With your expanded capabilities, you are prepared to learn practical business strategies to apply in your business.

Now you need to get into action mode. Because personal development means nothing without the action part. All three components—Personal Development, Business Strategies, and Daily Habits—are critical to having a healthy ecosystem.

PART TWO

business strategies

I F THERE is such a thing as a magic key to success, this step will provide you with the best "magic keys" I know of. What makes them magical is that these strategies are best suited to self-employed business owners.

We are not big business. We are probably not even big enough to be considered a small business. Our businesses are often relationally based, not transactional, like many businesses. We tend to be creative thinkers, so focusing on one thing and one audience, and following the all-too-frequent suggestion to find a niche isn't satisfying for us. Changes in the world, closer to home, and in the lives of our customers have a huge impact on us, making us more aware of what's going on around us and more empathetic to those we serve. How can we expect to do business like every other type of business? Marketing and building a successful self-employed business requires different marketing strategies and a different business model. This step is going to provide you with just what you need.

We crave ways of doing business that feel right and natural to us as self-employed business owners. Marketing strategies that don't feel creepy. A business model that is exciting and offers security in uncontrollable circumstances. A way of doing business that is creative, emotionally satisfying, and representative of our desire to serve. Hopefully, just like I felt when I was only fourteen years old selling eggs door-to-door, you'll become fascinated by the business side of being self-employed, as if it's one big magical puzzle.

When I was working with Marissa Polselli in my Small Business Consulting program, she wrote one day to say, "Today, I realized a fundamental shift in the way I understood my path as an entrepreneur. When you explained the concept of the Self-Employed Ecosystem, I felt myself let go of a breath I didn't know I was holding. And I began to embrace rather than fight against the natural rhythms and realities of self-employed life. I saw the interconnection between my capacity to grow my business and my personal development more clearly than ever before. I stopped trying to make this journey something it's not so I could revel in what it actually is. And I felt freer to lean into what my heart had already been telling me—that for me, it is all personal, and that's OK. In fact, it can be better than OK."

Marissa expressed what I see in my clients and on the faces of attendees at speaking events all the time. The look of relief. Finally, there's a way to do business as a self-employed business owner that feels good.

Imagine the impact on your business if you loved the business side! I believe that with the strategies you will learn in this next step, you will.

5

Embrace Hug Marketing

N THE final weeks of photography school, just as we were about to graduate and head out into the world, we had a guest speaker. He stood before us and said, "You're probably all leaving here broke students. As you set out to be a photographer, if you have limited funds and have to choose between buying yourself a camera and a telephone, buy the telephone." I don't think he offered much more than that by way of an explanation, but I totally got it. That one statement became foundational to how I feel about marketing.

As a guest on other people's podcasts, I've been asked questions of this nature, "If you were to move someplace where you knew no one and had only three hundred dollars and a laptop, what would you do?" My answer is always the same. I would take one hundred dollars and buy a decent mic for podcasting. With the remaining money, I would get a massage, take some yoga classes, and eat good food. For me, lifestyle always comes first.

Both scenarios show that marketing needs to be a priority. What good would it do to have the latest and greatest camera if I didn't have any customers? But with the telephone, I could drum up some business, even tell people I was booked weeks in advance, until which time I could fully book up my schedule. With a full schedule and the business that would be generated, I could afford the better camera. So yes, buy the telephone first. Buy the hammer before you try to drive in the nail. The car before the road trip. You get the idea. Understand what needs to come first in order to be successful at what you're setting out to accomplish.

Authentic Marketing

I have always made marketing a priority. It has to be, if you want business to go well. It also has to be done in a way that feels good for you so that you stick with it. The good news is, I believe marketing has evolved to be much more aligned with the behaviors and desires of most self-employed and small-business owners. It's much more expected now that marketing be honest, authentic, and transparent. When you *are* your business, how could this not be a better way to market your business? Many people used to think of marketing as dishonest, manipulative, and kind of gross. I mean, it wasn't that long ago that tobacco manufacturers were marketing cigarettes as cool and glamorous, knowing full well they were killing people. Of course, similar manipulative marketing continues today. But thankfully, consumers have a whole new standard. Minimally, consumers require honesty and transparency in marketing. If they find out otherwise, it's all over social media. Rightfully so. Or if there's a discrepancy between a brand's public image and how they treat their employees, it's not likely to stay a secret for very long. Decency is the minimum requirement in marketing today.

But we don't just want to meet the minimum requirement. To excel at marketing today, we need to move people emotionally—we want to get them from where they are, perhaps being strangers, to becoming customers. We want to engage them emotionally so they can make clear decisions about our products or services instead of being uncertain.

When you see it as your job to emotionally move people, you shift the responsibility of being successful from the customer to yourself, which gives you more control over your business. And it certainly feels better for your customer too. Emotionally engage them by sharing your values, your mission, and your stories. Make your customers feel like you "get" them. The goal in marketing today is to know your customers so well, they are likely to say, "Wow, it's like you're in my head." That's not just lead generation, it's forming a genuine bond. That's not a customer; it's a relationship. Now sales and marketing no longer feel creepy.

Relationship marketing like this is the sweet spot for the self-employed. It's what we're good at, and with little or no line between ourselves personally and our business, it's a joy to share ourselves authentically. This is why marketing has evolved to be more aligned with self-employment, offering an opportunity for you to enjoy marketing perhaps more than ever before. People want to do business with businesses that care.

The problem is, we still see plenty of examples of old-school manipulative marketing. It's possible no one has ever pointed out to you the fundamental ways in which marketing has changed so that you can embrace the new way to market. It's also possible that you have never been given specific marketing tips on exactly what works today that you can apply in your business. That's precisely what we are going to do in this chapter.

It's much more
expected now that
marketing be
**honest, authentic,
and transparent**.

———————————

Introducing Hug Marketing

You likely don't have an unlimited budget. Maybe you don't have *any* budget. That's not to say there's no money to spend on marketing. There may be. But you probably don't have a precise percentage that a committee has allotted for marketing based on extensive data that proves where the best return on investment is going to come from. No, we self-employed kind of wing it. Even if there is a budget of sorts, it's probably more like an intended range, subject to change at will because you can. Either way, the constraint of not having a budget without boundaries or not having enough can leave us without a concrete plan.

We need our marketing efforts to be efficient, streamlined, and manageable with a good return on investment because we don't have money to burn. We need specific efforts that lead to actual results. We need better results than just "getting the word out there." Rather than focusing on brand building and name recognition marketing, we're more likely to look at specific ways to market our business that bring recognizable results. Without big budgets, we need a more direct return on our efforts and investment.

Being a self-employed business owner and maybe a business of one, you are likely doing most, if not all, of your marketing yourself—trying to come up with fresh ideas to figure out how to express what you do for others. As I often say, one of the indicators that someone is an ideal customer for my Small Business Branding program is that they know they are good at what they do or are confident in the value of what they offer, but it seems others don't understand it. This is, of course, a huge problem in business. If people can't easily understand what you offer and see the exceptional value in it, why would they choose you? This is why marketing and brand message are so critical. You have to say the right things to the right people. The challenge is, we are so close to our own business that we can't see it objectively. If we can't see it objectively, we struggle to come up with the right things to say and get all tied up in a knot. My favorite expression about this is, "You can't read the label from inside the jar." As self-employed business owners, we are way inside the jar. How could we ever "read" the label and know the best way to market ourselves? Hopefully, you can hire a coach, consultant, or at least have a peer group that can objectively look at your business for you, so you can overcome one of the greatest struggles of marketing your own business.

There's also often misrepresentation of what is authentic about a business by the way it comes across. I call it a facade problem. We think we're supposed to present ourselves a certain way, so we do, but it doesn't reflect who we really are. In my brand message work, I see this all the time. When I review websites, I first have clients fill out an application with several questions about their business and who their ideal customer is. I ask, "Why do you do what you do?" and "What do you think are the top three values of your ideal customer?"

I ask these questions because people answer them from their heart. Reading the applications, I get a real sense of who they are, what's important to them, what's in their heart, and often how incredibly well they understand the emotions of their ideal customers. Then I go to the website, and 98 percent of the time, it feels nothing like what they wrote on the application. Not even close. Why is that? How is it that such a heart-centered, purpose-driven, customer-centric business can come across entirely different on its website? Usually, these misrepresentations are very flat, boring, and stale feeling. Or as I've been known to say, the website is a watered-down version of who they are.

I asked one client, "Do people often tell you you're polite?"

She said, "Yes. I've heard that my whole life. Why?"

I replied, "Because I read your application and it's powerful. Your website is very polite and, quite honestly, boring. Do you want to be bold and stand out, or polite and blend in?"

I believe this conformity is the result of feeling like there's a "right" way to come across. A professional facade. This is especially evident when you are in a particular trade. In some, there is an industry standard of how you're supposed to present yourself to stay aligned with the industry image. But if everyone fits the mold, how is anyone supposed to stand out?

Some of my favorite branding clients have been financial firms because there is definitely a way they believe they are supposed to come across. And it's boring! What I always have to point out to financial firms is that they are in one of the most emotionally charged businesses there is—money! How is it your marketing comes across so unemotional? It's because they have adopted the "supposed to look like" mentality of financial firms instead of being themselves.

One of my favorite financial firm clients was Susan Nieland. Susan's firm, CFO Solutions, presented itself in its marketing in just the way you'd expect from a financial firm: corporate-feeling, stiff, and boring. Of course, we wanted her to stand out. You can't imagine the difference on the CFO Solutions website when it went from typical and boring to emotionally evocative. The home page now features a photo of two thirty-somethings in a convertible driving into the sunset along the Pacific Coast. The woman has her arms stretched high in excitement because of the financial freedom they gained by having CFO Solutions take over their finances. You feel the emotions of financial freedom and making dreams come true the instant you land on the website. Much different from the former company logo, degrees, credentials, and bullet point list of services.

When you are your business, you must come across as truly who you are if you want to move people with your marketing.

As I said earlier, the whole point of marketing is to emotionally stir strangers enough that they become followers, and then leads, and, finally, customers. An even better way to say it: they go from stranger to fan, fan to bond, bond to relationship.

First, let's flip the script of how marketing is usually thought of and put it in better perspective. Once you get this idea down, you will make many other decisions regarding your marketing in a better way. It will also provide you with a clear path, making your marketing far more strategic and efficient. This concept can be your tool from which all of your marketing decisions are made.

When it comes to marketing, we typically hear terms like "marketing funnel"—meaning when one thing leads to another, which leads to another, and boom, you have a new client. Hopefully. I get it, but I hate the term. For that matter, a lot of marketing terms have a terrible energy to them that do not represent the energy of relationships we self-employed business owners need to have with our customers. We're the businesses where our customers become our friends and we know one another by name. Why on earth would we refer to our potential customers as a "target market" and welcome them in at the top of a funnel with lots of breathing room, only to squeeze them through a small hole as they get closer to becoming a customer?

In my own business, we have replaced the word "marketing" with "enrolling" because I don't even like the term "marketing." Marketing is usually followed by marketing *at* people or *to* people. Enrolling more accurately conveys what our objective is—to enroll clients into our services. To invite them to get closer to us. Not to market at them. If you try to market at people today, they back up.

If how you say something matters—and it does—let's stop calling the process of client acquisition a marketing funnel. Let's stop marketing from the energetic perspective of catching someone with a wide opening, like a Venus flytrap, only to squeeze them till we get what we want in the end. The shift in thinking from funnels and marketing *at* people to emotionally moving them toward purchase is a concept I call Hug Marketing. Make this your new advertising mantra and the way you do all of your promotion: *Embrace Hug Marketing*.

Instead of a funnel, with a wide opening at the top and a smaller opening at the bottom, Hug Marketing can be illustrated by a series of concentric circles, or rings—one inside the other, each circle being slightly smaller, until you get to the center, or what we're going to call "the hug."

Each circle represents the current state of relationship you have with the individual who will hopefully become a client, and an action you need to take to emotionally move a prospective customer to the next circle.

Let's say there are six circles. (The number of circles will depend on your business and your journey to a "hug." In general, the higher the ticket item, the more circles it can take to move someone from where they are to investing in your services or product.) We'll start with the outermost circle and move inward.

- Lurkers
- Curious
- Engaged
- Connected
- Client
- Hug

Lurkers

The outermost circle contains people who are watching you from afar, perhaps on social media, but who don't follow you yet. Or they have found their way to you through a search. Listeners of *The Self-Employed Life* podcast, for example, are in this outer circle to start. They are there, but I don't know them yet. This is the true value of social media and having a podcast—to get eyeballs (or ears!) on you and your business. Other than advertising on social media, the primary goal is not a direct return on investment. This is why business owners so often get frustrated and think there's no value in social media; they don't see an immediate result because the people are not yet committed to connecting—they're just lurking.

Curious

The next circle is of those who have taken the step of following you on social media. You connect on LinkedIn; they begin to follow you on Instagram; they follow your Facebook business page; maybe they send a friend request or subscribe to your podcast. You may find that when this person is inspired to step into this circle, they connect with you on multiple platforms at once. It might even feel a little stalkerish. In a good way. Something about you and your business struck them, so they are stepping in to find out more. They are curious.

Engaged

Once connected, you may find the people start to interact with you. They like your posts, share your content, and start to comment. They have now stepped another circle in. They may stay here for a while, even years. This is when the relationship really begins to build. Be patient and genuine. The biggest mistake you can make in this process and all your marketing is to rush the relationship. What would happen if you started talking about marriage and having kids on a first date? Most of us would completely freak out. I know, I know, you're an impatient business owner. But believe me, you will be rewarded for having patience and building a genuine relationship. In this circle, the people are engaged.

Connected

In the next circle, or at the next level of the acquisition process, the potential customer signs up for your mailing list, for example, likely the result of some content you've offered—or what is typically called a lead magnet. But the lead magnet needs to provide real value because there's really nothing free about it. If people have to surrender an email address, they know that comes with a price. They'd better love your content, or they will opt out. Being a guest on podcasts is also excellent for relationship building and moving along these circles quickly if you offer value in the conversation and a way for the listener to opt in to your email list, because you've offered something they really want. Once in this circle, they are now connected.

Client

Once they're on your email list, you can and should engage with them in a more personal manner. It's in this circle of direct relationship with you through email marketing, your newsletter, or your blog that they step up and hire you or buy your product. Now they are a customer or client.

Hug

Think you're done? Nope. One more step. That's the hug, at the center of the circles. Having built a solid relationship by moving them emotionally through a series of circles, and having delivered on your promise with your service or product, they love you! And you love them! This is when they become loyal customers, advocates for your work, and sources of referrals. They are huggers.

I think you'll find that a six-circle Hug Marketing journey is sufficient for the majority of businesses. However, as I mentioned, a higher-ticket item may require an additional circle or two. Perhaps a phone call or in-person meeting. If it's a lower-priced item with less risk, they may bypass much of the process and jump right in. Carefully consider your offer in order to decide the number of circles it will require for them to go from the distance of a lurker to the center of a hug.

What I also love about the energy of Hug Marketing is that it puts the burden of responsibility on you as the business owner. Knowing that it's your job to walk a prospective client through all these circles, doesn't it make you take more care and put in more conscious effort? Even more importantly, doesn't it feel more like who you are? Hug Marketing can take the creepy out of marketing and the salesy out of sales, and remove the pressure to be someone you're not. To me, that is the greatest benefit of embracing Hug Marketing.

6

Create an
Emotional Journey

SINCE RELEASING *LINGO* in 2018, I have come to realize that brand message and saying the right things to the right people in the right sequence is even more critical than I realized when I wrote the book. I mean, I knew brand message was important or I wouldn't have written it. But I was more focused on you saying the right things to the right people to attract your ideal customers. What I came to realize once *LINGO* was out there was that the sequence in which you deliver your message is every bit as important. Hence the development of the emotional journey.

Summarizing the key point in one of my favorite books, *Louder Than Words*, by my friend Todd Henry, the energy of how you say something is often more important, louder, than the words themselves. Isn't that the truth? You can completely change how something you say feels to the recipient based on how you say it. My ex-mother-in-law, whom I loved dearly, was masterful at making you realize you had been insulted after the fact. Because how she delivered her message sounded good... until you thought about it.

We also know that in life, timing is often everything. Now you'll see that it's not just *what* you say or even *how* you say it, but also *when* you say it.

The journey on which you take visitors, whether it's prospective customers on your website, readers of your blog, or listeners of your podcast, is a blend of consumer behavior psychology and the subtleties of your audience. For example, typical consumer behavior will say that people need to see their problem before they seek a solution. As a general rule, I would say that is true. However, the nuance is, how do you point out the problem so that your audience responds well? Is it the usual—pointing out their pain approach? Or is it more aspirational, helping them imagine what is possible if their pain point is solved? More than in the past, I think many people prefer an aspirational message.

So, this idea of knowing the emotional journey your audience needs to go on in order to buy into your offer means understanding them on a whole new level. Yes, it still about the message—their lingo. It's also about the sequence in which they need to receive it.

Let's start with understanding what's changed and why brand message is more important than ever.

Why Your Brand Message Is More Important Than Ever

Here are just a few reasons:

Buyers want shared values. In today's day and age, who someone chooses to do business with is based on an alignment of values, an emotional connection, and whether they feel the business or brand "gets" them. Phew, this is good for us self-employed people, who are good at emotional connection. We just have to share ourselves.

Over my thirty-five years in business, I have seen this transition from impersonal to personal firsthand. In the past, being the best in your field or having name recognition used to be the primary driver for someone to choose you. As a photographer in the eighties and nineties serving families with impeccably decorated homes, it was amazing to me how often my clients would tell me about their diva interior designer who was driving them crazy but, "you know, he/she is the designer to have." So, they made a choice to work with the designer who had the most prestigious name and was undoubtedly extremely talented, but also had an attitude.

I'm not going to take the designers' talents away from them. Without talent, it's unlikely they would have achieved that name recognition. But try to get away with that today! It's not enough to be considered "the best." People don't hire you because you're the best. They hire you because they feel like you understand them and their needs, desires, and goals. We hire people we like, and get rid of them if we don't. Talent and being good at what you do or produce is important. But you're not going to get by on talent, skill set, or quality alone anymore. Now, we buy products or services from brands that we feel align with our values, sometimes even at a higher price.

REI, the outdoor recreation retailer, has a devoted following of customers because it not only offers quality products but also closes its stores every year on Black Friday, the biggest retail day of the year, to encourage staff and customers to get outside instead of being at the mall or in front of a computer online shopping. REI is walking its talk and living its mission as an outdoor recreation company.

I'm a huge fan of Seventh Generation, which sells eco-friendly cleaning, paper, and personal care products, because of our shared value of the environment. I'm willing to pay a bit more to do the right thing. I also buy my shoes primarily from Fluevog. Not only are the shoes exceptionally well designed, but also I live for the inspiring messages that come on the shoe bags and in their packaging. The company's special touch reflects what both of us value.

In response to a social media post I made about this topic, Elizabeth Anne Hamilton, partner at Another Big Production, expressed her devotion to Lush, the cosmetics retailer, this way: "They prioritize doing the right thing over profits. All their products are made using workers who are paid living wages. They use supplies that are sustainably sourced, and I'm willing to pay more to know they are made justly." Powerful, isn't it? Don't you want to be that to your customers?

Penzeys Spices, the largest independent spice retailer in the United States, has become a brand known not only for its outstanding quality of spices but also for the very vocal opinions of the founder, Bill Penzey. He completely debunks the theory that business is business and politics should be left out. The more vocal and direct he is in sharing his opinion of politics, the more enamored he seems to become among fans of the company. Swati Jagetia, a mental health counselor and executive coach, said, "They have a voice and they use it. They are willing to stand up for people and risk losing business. [In fact, it's had the opposite effect.] And they promote kindness above all."

While mission statements, value statements, and a founder's story are helpful for big business, nothing compares to sharing values, your "why," and your story when you are your own business. If your customers or people interacting with your brand for the first time feel emotional resonance, they will choose you. That's why brand message is more important than ever.

Knowing the emotional journey your audience needs to go on in order to buy into your offer means **understanding them on a whole new level**.

It's harder now to get people's attention. Two of the best things you can do in business are to not blame others, and to take responsibility for what you need to do to overcome challenges. It does no good to blame a so-called lack of attention for why you are not getting customers. It's better to overcome the challenge. Sure, data exists to support the idea that smartphones have made us, well, less smart. But how does knowing that help? Does it actually solve the problem? If we take complete responsibility rather than lay blame, we might realize the issue is less about people not having an attention span and perhaps more that our brand is not attention-worthy. Also, with so many distractions, people have rightfully become attention snobs!

Given a choice between the latest hit series on Netflix or your website, which do you think people would choose? Your website would have to be pretty compelling to pull my attention from Netflix, if I were watching a movie with my laptop in front of me, and inspire me to call someone else's attention to it. Have you ever found something so captivating that you stopped what you were doing and interrupted someone else to show them too? Imagine passing the Netflix test and being so attention-worthy that you distracted them, at least enough to hit pause.

They are self-vetting. Typically, people are already 50 to 70 percent convinced they'll choose you before they even reach out to your business. What do you think they are using to make that decision? Your brand message and image! This is what I refer to as doing business in the Age of Empowerment, when consumers have all the power and tools to choose who they want to do business with. Isn't this what you want too? To be empowered to make your own decisions? The moment you try to take that power away, potential consumers back up.

There's both good and bad news in knowing people are 50 to 70 percent on their way to choosing you before they've even reached out. The good news is that you just have to confirm the decision they've already made! Don't screw it up and you're good. The bad news is, that's a lot of pressure to make sure your brand message resonates. This is why, to get and keep their attention, what you say and how you say it are so important.

Mobile usage dominates. Years ago, website technology became responsive so that websites built for desktops would easily translate to mobile devices. At the same time, somehow marketers and businesses didn't respond to the fact that people behave differently on a mobile device. Numerous studies have shown that the majority of people interacting with your brand are on mobile devices. Depending on who your ideal customer is, it could be considerably higher or a little lower. If your ideal customers are millennials, it could be 10 to 14 percent higher. Gen Z knows nothing but life on a mobile device.

Also, often our best customers are on the go and busy, the proverbial movers and shakers who, in many cases, have discretionary income. Busy lifestyle = increased mobile usage. So today, to attract your ideal customers, you want to think about the mobile user.

The main obstacle we face is that people on mobile devices are reluctant to go to interior pages on a website. They load too slowly, and, hey, there isn't even a proper menu, just the hamburger menu with its three lines. Nothing about a website on a mobile device encourages a visitor to go to an interior page. If they need to, say, for shopping on an e-commerce site, it's only after they are really compelled to do so by the home page. The home page on your website is everything today. That's why in a moment I'm going to share perhaps one of my most valuable marketing strategies.

The point is, because visitors to your website are likely to never leave the home page unless really motivated to do so, the brand message on your home page has to be killer—instantly compelling to get their attention—and provide everything they need to know to choose you.

For the purpose of learning about brand messaging, to take your prospective customers from being lurkers to huggers, we're going to focus on your website, specifically the home page. After learning this process, many people apply this emotional journey to all of their marketing materials and content, including sales pages, emails, blogs, and other marketing.

OK, that really valuable marketing strategy I promised you? Here it is.

The Emotional Journey Website Map

Considering the home page on your website, I look at brand messaging initially as having two big parts. The first part is what I refer to as the opening scene—what is first seen by the visitor when your website loads. It may or may not be all of what is "above the fold," which is what is seen on a device prior to scrolling. On a mobile device, you are almost certainly going to have to scroll in order to see the entire opening scene.

The opening scene must be super-compelling and make the customer you are trying to attract feel as if they have just landed in paradise, or at least in the right place. You get my drift: it has to be a showstopper.

The second big part is everything you say after that and the order in which you say it. This is very important because we are emotional buyers. While there are some generalizations that can be made about the sequence of content for human behavior, it's important to adapt the sequence based on your ideal audience.

Emotional Journey of Your Customer

THE LOOK AND FEEL

Emotional trigger: Style
What they are saying: "I'm in the right place"

IMAGES, COLORS, FONTS

CREATES THE CONNECTION

Emotional trigger: Familiarity
What they are saying: "You're speaking to me"

STAND OUT STATEMENT
(MAY ALSO BE ON IMAGES)

POINTS OUT THEIR PROBLEMS

Emotional trigger: Understanding
What they are saying: "It's like you're in my head"

SELF-IDENTIFYING
QUESTIONS

HOW YOU CAN HELP THEM

Emotional trigger: Craving
What they are saying: "I need that"

THE BENEFITS OF
YOUR OFFER

HOW IT WORKS

Emotional trigger: Trust
What they are saying: "I trust you"

YOUR PROCESS

YOUR AUTHORITY

Emotional trigger: Relatability
What they are saying: "It's no wonder this is what you do"

ABOUT

I find it helpful to understand these two big sections before creating the overall objective of the brand message on your home page. Get your prospective customers' attention; stop them in their tracks; make them feel they are in the right place. Take them on a complete journey of getting everything they need to choose you. Or, as I often say, take them from compelled to contact as quickly as possible.

Understanding the objective, let's break it down by section, keeping in mind that we want the visitor to experience the sequence like a series of sections flowing seamlessly together.

Opening Scene

Think of the opening scene on the home page as your only opportunity to make an amazing first impression. The opening scene has two primary components—a representative, evocative image and a Stand Out Statement. The Stand Out Statement is your core brand message, which lets the visitor know *what* and *whom* your brand stands for and is so compelling it *stands out*! You can look at it as the modern-day version of a slogan or tagline. The difference is, your Stand Out Statement will have an energy to it and mean something to your ideal customers.

Jamie Mustard, author of *The Iconist: The Art and Science of Standing Out*, stresses the importance of a bold brand statement, what he calls a Block, this way: "Anyone communicating in any medium must consciously and deliberately lead with a big, bold, simple Block as the first point of contact if they want to be seen."

Your Stand Out Statement needs to not only be compelling, but also keep their attention, for which you typically have only a few seconds. Your Stand Out Statement must be three to nine words, as that's all the time you have to get their attention, and you have a lot to say! You can also think of it as a book title and subtitle. Your three- to nine-word Stand Out Statement can be supported with subtext, like the subtitle of a book. The title gets the attention, the subtitle provides the context.

My Stand Out Statement is "Small Business. Big Dreams." You know who I stand for—small business—and what I stand for—big dreams. Four words that say a lot. My subtitle is "Business Strategies and Personal Development for Self-Employed Business Owners." There's no question whom I serve and what I do. That's what an effective Stand Out Statement does in your opening scene.

There's no one way to develop your Stand Out Statement. It's the deep work of understanding your customers' values, lifestyle, expectations, and what interests them. For clients of my Small Business Branding program, it's often the last thing we develop, even though it's the first thing seen on the website. That's because it really does come from within the process of learning about your customer. It comes from knowing them deeply and finding a way to bring that core message to the surface. When you "get it," that statement that just feels so right to you and that you know is an attention-grabber for your ideal customers, it goes boldly in the opening scene, often over an image.

The image of the opening scene also has to be relatable to the audience and the message. The implied message of the image is often one of the biggest miscommunications I see on a website. It must support the Stand Out Statement and be meaningful to your ideal customer. I consulted with a business owner once who described her work as coaching affluent, middle-aged women going through a divorce. I had to ask her, then, why the image in her opening scene was a thirty-something-year-old woman dancing in a field. She certainly wasn't middle-aged and her ideal client sure as hell doesn't feel like dancing in a field right now! (She didn't hire me... go figure.) It sounds ridiculous doesn't it? But I see breaks like this all the time. A brand message of friendly and excellent service over a photo that is stiff and cold, or that poorly reflects what the company does and what it stands for. A company portraying themselves as a calm solution over a video of cars chaotically zipping by on a highway does not resonate. The image must be a continuation of the Stand Out Statement and relatable in all characteristics to your ideal customer.

Lead Magnet

The next section after the opening scene is likely to be a lead magnet. A lead magnet is content or a service that offers prospective customers a sample of your value. It could be informative, such as a how-to guide; helpful like a top tips list; or supportive, like my website brand message review. While a lead magnet can come in many forms, one thing is for certain: it must provide value for the prospect. They know they have to surrender their email. That's what makes it a lead for you. But for them, that's not free, so high value is a must. You also want to be creative. Once lead magnets became a popular marketing strategy, everyone was doing the same thing. Remember free PDF books? Which brings up another point—it must be how people see value in the current day. Hardly anyone wants an extensive in-depth PDF today. It's too much. That's why the top-ten-tip sort of lead magnets have become popular, or the five steps. Self-assessments can be very effective as a lead magnet.

Another key factor in your lead magnet is that it must be aligned with the services you offer. It is, after all, intended to lead someone from being engaged to being connected on the Hug Marketing journey. Think of a lead magnet as a sampling, or a taste, of what you offer. I like to imagine my prospective coaching client experiencing my sample of work and thinking, "Wow! If I got this from him now, imagine what it would be like to work with him one-on-one!"

Empowerment Section

This section is critical in the sequence of the emotional journey. Remember, you just got your potential client's attention. Now, as they scroll a bit, the empowerment section should emotionally hook them; this is when they realize for themselves that you "get" them.

It is in this section that the deep work of understanding the intimate details of your customers pays off. Here, you pose questions or make statements that ring so true for your ideal customers that they can't help but wonder if you are in their head. Or in their bedroom.

Let me explain. OgallalaComfort.com, a branding client of mine, produces the most wonderful comforters and pillows using a blend containing milkweed. While there are many exceptional attributes to milkweed, one is that it's more breathable than most bedding materials. With your body temperature more controlled, you are less likely to experience night sweats and chills.

During one of our meetings, I asked, "Do any of you sleep with one foot outside the comforter?" Sheepishly, hands went up. Mine included. I knew they were thinking, "This is a weird question..." Truth is, this is like my version of a party game. I ask audiences and groups this all the time as an example of just how specific a question can be. In fact, the more specific, the better, because it shows you know them. As it turns out, many people sleep with one foot outside the comforter; it helps us moderate body temperature. We may like the weight and warmth of the comforter, but a chilly foot cools us down.

So, on their website, in the empowerment section, the copy says Ogallala comforters are "so breathable you don't have to stick your foot out." I've always wanted to see the faces of customers when they read that! What I do know is that sales went up 30 percent from the previous year when the website

If your customers or people interacting with your brand for the first time feel emotional resonance, **they will choose you**.

---

launched. I suspect their level of intimacy contributed to their customers feeling understood, hence the increase in sales.

What questions could you ask that speak precisely to the state of mind or current condition of your ideal customers? What statements might you make that ring entirely true for them? What pains do you know to be true for them because maybe you've been there too? How about dreams and aspirations you may have in common that maybe they've never shared with someone else?

Posing well-thought-out questions and statements will make them feel like you get them, and your powerful insights into who they are will make them feel confident in choosing you. The empowerment section is the most important part of your home page. When you get this right, it's a game changer.

As you might imagine, by this point, the visitor to your website is considerably emotionally committed. Now, they just want to validate in their mind what their heart is already saying (enter whisper in ear, "Do it!").

Benefits Section

For your potential customer to overcome that pesky logical part of the brain, now you want to point out the benefits of choosing you. The benefits section is a twofold process. First, point out the benefits of what you do or offer in a more general sense. For example, the benefit of having a coach is knowing there's always someone to guide and advise you. So, you're not specifically pointing out the benefit of choosing you yet. I often refer to the benefits section also as the romance section because you are wooing your prospective clients with all that is possible with what you offer. You might start a sentence or two with "Imagine..." Get them to paint a picture in their mind of all that is possible. You're helping the heart tell the brain to "hold my beer; I've got this."

Next, you point out the specific benefits of choosing you. What makes you different, uniquely qualified? Point out your experience and education—but please, no résumés. Here, you provide heartfelt expressions of what makes you the best choice for them. Not just anyone—for them specifically. For example, it's in this section on my website that I point out how being a photographer for decades has shown me the power of making people feel seen. How I can help you understand your customers so well they will feel completely seen, heard, and understood, and when they do, they will choose you, often regardless of price. I point out that I offer a completely different perspective as a photographer turned small-business and brand message consultant. This is also a good place to include testimonials and endorsements.

I want to call something to your attention here: Do you see how long it is on the website before you talk about yourself? Until this moment of revealing the benefits of choosing you, it's been all about the visitor to the website. That is, after all, the point—this is about them. Far too many websites are salesy, "all about me" online brochures. They need to be all about the customer first.

Process Section

At this point, the prospective customer's voice of reason wants to chime in: "But how do I know this is the right choice?" I'll tell you. It is here in the process section that you lightly review your process, whether it's a service process or a manufacturing process. Basically, a very light version of how you do what you do. We want this to be the light version because you want to give just enough explanation that their voice of reason knows this is not your first rodeo. At this point, you are confirming your experience and building trust. You can do this with paragraphs, steps, bullet points, or graphics. We don't want to overwhelm them. Too many businesses are so proud of their process that they provide way too much information about how they do what they do. Keep the explanation of your process simple. You simply want to set aside any final concerns before moving on to the all-important next section.

Authority Section

As you near the end of your website, you're going to include the very important authority section. I like to refer to this as "ending with why." You may be familiar with Simon Sinek's book *Start with Why*. It's a fantastic concept and I have the utmost respect for Simon. However, when it comes to your website, I prefer to end with "why." Let me explain.

At this point in their emotional journey, your potential customers have been compelled; their heart has already made its decision and they feel like you understand them; you gave the logical brain what it needs to know to quiet down, and their voice of reason heard just enough to trust you. Now they are just about ready to choose you.

The idea of the authority section is to share your "why"— the story behind why this work is meaningful to you. It can be a bit of a founder's story, but it is not an About page. It's just a paragraph or two, a heartfelt explanation or story behind why you do what you do. For example, on my website, I share the story of my Waffle Sundays. Although it's a personal endeavor, it explains who I am and what I value, which is also reflected in my business. The definitive goal of the authority section is for the prospective client to think, "Oh, it's no wonder this is what you do!" Up until now, it's been all about you understanding them. Now, they understand you. The relationship is sealed. They see you as not only the best choice, but also the only choice.

Contact Form

One final but important step. Every home page needs to end with an embedded contact form. Super-simple. You just need space for their name, email, and maybe a note. Don't make them go back to the top menu and click on a contact page. Nope, have it right there, at the bottom of the page, so they can immediately follow their heart. Remember, this is an emotional journey, from start to finish.

Keep in mind that while the Emotional Journey Website Map is a solid structure for your home page, it should still be expressed in your brand voice and style. Use images, graphics, fonts, and design elements throughout to make sure it is uniquely yours. The last thing I want to create is a template that makes every website look the same. While the map is divided into sections for ease of understanding, each section should flow seamlessly to the next. This is about how it feels on the inside for the visitor to your site. It should be stylized in your own unique way.

The reason I am openly sharing such valuable and proprietary information, which until now was available only to clients, is that I want this work to change lives and the world. Yes, your life, because you'll grow your business, but also the lives of those you serve by making them feel seen. It will just be a better world, and that's reason enough for me.

However, you are in business to support your life. Therefore, you need a solid business model, which is what we're going to cover next.

7

Build a Business Model of Multiples

T O NICHE or not to niche, that is the question. There seem to be as many opinions on whether or not to create a niche business as there are people who have opinions on how to pronounce niche—like quiche or like ditch? Personally, I prefer to pronounce it as "nitch" so I can say things like, "Ditch the niche," because that's how I feel about it. However you pronounce it, I'm talking about being known for doing one specific thing, maybe even for one specific audience.

Now, before anyone gets all bent out of shape (because there are always some who do), allow me to clarify. For some, picking a niche makes perfect sense—as some say, "the riches are in the niches." Heck, my photography business was about as niche as they come—traditional-style posed portraits in color for affluent families. It was literally a niche for the rich. But I started that business in the eighties, when such a business model made sense. It was the age of specialization, when we no longer went to general practitioners for anything, say, the family doctor. Instead, we went to experts in specific fields, such as a different doctor for each body part. It was pre-Internet, there was less competition for attention, and there seemed to be more than enough business to go around. Under those circumstances, you could afford to go narrow. Again, this still works for some.

But this book is for you, my ideal reader, and I'm willing to bet the idea of doing one thing for one audience feels stifling. Even boring. As some have said to me, "That would be the death of me."

Gain Control of Your Business

If not a niche, what is it? If not a business model of doing one thing for one group of people, what kind of business model is it? I've heard everything from a portfolio business model to a diverse business model. I like to refer to it as a Business Model of Multiples.

It comes down to this. If there is to be a niche, it's not the one thing you *do*. It's the one thing you *are known for*. Your area of expertise. But this "area" is spacious and has breathing room. Your area of expertise is your core brand message and Stand Out Statement.

How is this different from the traditional niche? Well, it's not about being limited to doing one thing; it's about being known for one thing for which there are multiple audiences and multiple ways you can do that thing. That's what makes it a Business Model of Multiples. Plus, by having a Business Model of Multiples, you can have multiple streams of income.

Doesn't that feel freeing? For years, after I spoke on this topic at events, attendees would often come up to me, excitedly shake my hand, and say, "Thank you! I feel like you gave me permission." At first, I had no idea what that meant. I politely smiled back and probably said something like, "I'm glad it resonated for you." (Because that sounds like something a coach would say, right?) After having this happen time and again, I finally realized they were feeling as if I'd given them permission to be in business in a way that feels good to them. Before, they had probably been told that the riches are in the niches, and that in order to succeed, they had to pick a niche and home in. I guess my perspective was freeing to them.

I get it. I remember the exact moment I gave myself permission to stop listening to others and listen to what made sense to me. What made sense to me then, and even more so today, was to have a Business Model of Multiples.

We left the eighties behind, along with big hair, Pac-Man, phones tethered to the wall, and waiting in line to see *E.T.* Back then, it was easier to stand out, and specialization commanded a higher price. But times have changed, and so have customers and business. That's why we also need to leave the old definition of niche behind.

Today, in a fast-changing world, if you do just one thing for one audience, anything can come along to make you obsolete. Talk about potentially being the victim of uncontrollable circumstances! Even a single piece of technology can come along to make your primary industry irrelevant.

Take the invention of the GPS. As you might suspect, the convenience of the GPS through various apps such as Google Maps has had a major impact on the world's leading paper mapmaker, Rand McNally. By the time the fourth-generation family-owned business sold to AEA Investors in 1997, the mapping industry was already being completely transformed by modern technology. With paper maps being their core business model, and not having stayed ahead of technology change, the company ultimately ended up going bankrupt and closing all their retail stores. (Did you even know they had retail stores? I didn't.)

But the story doesn't end there. The resilient spirit of the founders, William Rand and Andrew McNally—who saved their business in 1871 by burying two printing machines in the sandy shores of Lake Michigan during the Great Chicago Fire that destroyed the city—must live on in the company today. Rand McNally has since saved itself once again. Their Business Model of Multiples offers navigation, headphones for truck drivers and such, educational materials to teach geography, and, yes, they still sell paper maps. Apparently, there are people who still like to suffer trying to fold a map!

Not only is a Business Model of Multiples more stimulating, and not only does it protect you from becoming obsolete, but it also gives you more control. Remember that why you went into business for yourself was to have control over your life and destiny? A Business Model of Multiples gives you about as much control over your business, income, and destiny as you're ever going to get.

We saw this firsthand during the COVID-19 pandemic and the shutdown of many businesses and events. The virus's restrictions wreaked havoc on the speaking industry. One by one, events were canceled or rescheduled for virtual attendance. Those speakers whose entire income was based on speaking live in front of an audience began to panic. Because they tended to speak at the biggest events and often commanded the highest fees, they were the most vulnerable. Of course, the largest events fell first, and they will be the last to come back (at the time of this writing, the pandemic and its constraints are ongoing after a year). This has left the highest-paid speakers who were the most reliant on speaking for their income in the most difficult position. *Ouch.*

But those speakers who had diverse offerings already built into their business model were able to adapt quicker. Perhaps in addition to speaking they offer consulting services or have a course to sell. For many in this situation, the pandemic has actually strengthened their business in that they have been able to expand on what they had already created. But to have to start from nothing to suddenly create streams of income when the primary stream dries up is extremely challenging, and may not make up the gap in income as quickly as you need it. (And then there's the personal toll it takes on you to find yourself in that position.)

This is the greatest lesson and reason to have a Business Model of Multiples. This is how you gain and maintain control over your business and destiny. Imagine your Business Model of Multiples like standing before a control panel of levers. You are in control of which levers get pulled down or pushed up. It's your choice. If a lever gets yanked down by circumstances outside of your business, you are at least in control of what levers you push up. Or you can pull down a lever in order to devote more time to, or push up, another lever. The key is having choice. Choice gives you control.

Not all levers are pulled down quickly. If you are in a corporate job and you dream of someday being self-employed full time, you can amp up the lever of your side hustle a bit. Little by little, you give it more time and more energy while at the same time maybe you pull down the lever on the full-time job. I have coached numerous professionals through this process of transitioning from full time for someone else to full time for themselves. Similarly, when I introduced coaching and speaking and later consulting, and then writing books and hosting a podcast, to my photography business, it gave me a lot of control in deciding which levers I lifted up and which I pulled down. I took it slow and gradually committed less and less time to being a photographer and more time to the other areas that were my future.

With a Business Model of Multiples, if there are sudden changes in your work or in the world that impact your business, you can be much quicker on your feet and perhaps find yourself thriving when others are simply trying to survive.

Steps to Building Your Business Model of Multiples

Your Area of Expertise

How might you discover your expanded services and products? First, get clear on your area of expertise. If it's not clearly and easily identifiable to you, it certainly won't be to anyone else.

Here's an exercise. Imagine you're walking down the sidewalk in Anytown, USA. As you walk by two people having a conversation, you overhear one say to the other, "Oh, so-and-so [insert your name or business], she's the go-to expert for _____."

How would you fill in the blank? If you can't, neither can anyone else. And it has to be easy and in normal conversation. For example, no one is going to say, "Oh, Mary, she's the go-to expert for finding your purpose and getting paid what you're worth." They will say, "Oh, Mary, she's the go-to expert for career coaching."

How you describe your area of expertise is not a marketing line. It's real talk—how someone would speak about you. That's the first step in building your business of multiples.

Understand What Makes You Different

The second step is to understand what makes you different. Is it your process? Perhaps it's your unique perspective—how you approach what you do differently from how others do it.

A Business Model of Multiples

gives you about as much control over your business, income, and destiny as you're ever going to get.

Hardly any of us are alone in our fields. But why you do what you do, your philosophies and background story, and how you look at what you do cannot be matched by anyone. Combined, these things are what make you different. Or maybe it's your past work experience that gives you a unique understanding of the problems and solutions you can offer. Perhaps it's a combination of past work experiences. A client of mine, business strategist Tamika Stewart, is a licensed therapist who also has decades of experience as an executive in mid-level companies. This creates a unique blend of therapy to break through your blocks, and strategies to create your business plan. If you want to get out of your own way and get on your way to a better future, Tamika, with her no-nonsense style, is the one to hire.

Grow with Multiple Audiences

Once you know your area of expertise and what makes you stand out, you can ask: What groups of people would love what I offer? This is the third step to building your business model.

This is when you think about your multiples. For example, for Tamika, we determined that those who would most love her services were:

1. **Start-ups:** Particularly those led by younger leaders needing clear direction, not wanting to waste time.

2. **Midlife entrepreneurs:** People wanting to leave their full-time job to pursue a dream, who need not only a solid action plan but also the support that her training as a therapist provides to get past the fears and obstacles inherent in such a big life change.

3. **Executives:** Perhaps they want to hone their skills for career advancement or are struggling to find happiness with where they are.

It doesn't need to be an exhaustive list, but as in this case, even starting with three audiences you can serve gives you tremendous control without feeling like you're all over the place. You will likely find that serving your multiple audiences will be a seamless process, because although they may have different starting points, what they need and your process are going to be quite similar.

Expand with Multiple Services

Now that you have multiple audiences, you can think about the myriad ways you can deliver your services: in person, virtually, through online courses, in books, with workshops and retreats, and so on. Really, the list is endless. Think of yourself like a versatile artist who creates their art using different media. You can be the same. Multiple audiences and several ways of delivering your services make a Business Model of Multiples.

Let's build yours:

Your area of expertise

"Oh, _____ [your name or name of business], they are the go-to expert for _____ [your area of expertise]."

What makes you different

What makes me different is [could be your process, your background, work experience, educational experiences, life experience, and how you see what you do differently]:

_____

_____

_____

_____

_____

_____

Your audiences

Make a list of those who would love what you offer:

People who _____

People who _____

People who _____

People who _____

People who _____

People who _____

Your media

Make a list of the various ways you can deliver your services:

_____

_____

_____

_____

_____

_____

_____

What I prefer about this model over the idea of pivoting is that it's not necessarily about a change of direction, as a pivot often implies. It's about expansion and more possibilities for income. For creative-thinking self-employed business owners who often feel as if they are being pulled in many directions, the Business Model of Multiples gives them choices and control of their direction.

With the choices available to you, there are now several "levers"—going back to my control panel scenario—that you can push up or pull down at your discretion to see your way through almost all circumstances. The following graphic shows the various levers in my business.

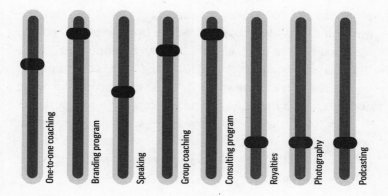

My business model is built around a single audience: self-employed business owners. But I have several services, which leads to seven to eight different income streams. This gives me control at all times to decide which levers I want to ramp up and which I want to pull down a little or completely. For years, I've been slowly pulling down the lever of photography. Not that I don't love it, but I've gone as far as I wanted as a photographer and work now only with select past clients. I've moderated the lever of one-to-one coaching a bit because it's very time heavy, whereas I've strongly ramped up the levers of small-business consulting and small-business branding, where I can create a huge impact for my clients in a short period of time, allowing me to accomplish more. It's all about control of your business.

In order to not get spread too thin, I find most businesses operate best with no more than seven to eight income streams. You can have distinctly different audiences with services for each and some services for more than one audience. For example, my fellow speaker friend Denise Jacobs has four different audiences—creatives, leaders of companies, mid-level executives, and entry-level executives. As a speaker, she has one income stream that can reach each of these groups in different ways. She also has LinkedIn Learning courses that reach creatives and entry-level executives, her own Amplify-U course designed for mid-level career folks, and her individual coaching reserved for mid-level executives and leaders of companies. So, she has four income streams that reach one or more of her audiences, creating a diverse and empowering business model.

Now, let's make sure you have all the systems in place to put your actions to good use. Many of these systems will be brand-new to you. This is how we get you what you want in an easier way than ever before.

8

Set Up Systems for Success

EVERY SUMMER when I was growing up, my family would spend a week or more camping on a lake in the Adirondacks of New York State. Adirondack Park is about 2.3 million acres of pristine protected land that never seemed to change over the years. Every year, from as early as I can remember until I was twenty-seven years old, it was an annual family tradition to go camping there with my five cousins and their families.

There were sandbars that jutted out into the peaceful lake. We would set up for the day on a sandbar with our chairs and blankets, ready for a fun day in the sun. Being a loner as a child, my absolute favorite thing to do was to dig in the sand while the other kids ran off with a floaty or something. I'd take a plastic shovel and dig a hole as deep as I could a few feet from the edge of the water. The thrill was when I'd dig down so far, I'd hit water. Remember thinking you could dig to China? Not going to say I didn't wonder.

Once I'd dug a hole as deep as I could, I'd carve a channel in the sand from the hole I dug all the way to the water's edge. That's when what seemed like magic would happen. I'd watch in wonder as the water ran down my newly created channel and filled in the reservoir. Somehow this nerdy little activity kept me occupied for hours and was a never-ending source of fascination for me year after year. Well, until I got old enough to find interest in pre-teen things.

Looking back, I realize my fascination lay in the idea of creating space and seeing it fill up. With a shovel and sand, I yielded the power to make that happen.

Today, the concept still fascinates me. This idea of making space and watching it get filled up is foundational to success and the systems of your business. It's also foundational to what makes the Self-Employed Ecosystem work. To refer back to Jim Rohn's quote yet again (because it's that good): "Your level of success will rarely exceed your level of personal development."

This is really about capacity. As you develop yourself personally, you increase the capacity of success that you are prepared for so that more success can come into your life. You and your business are like the reservoir in the sand, and the incoming flow of water is your incoming business and the life you want to live.

That's why the systems you need for your business, some traditional and some not, should be for the business you want, not the business you currently have. Too often, the systems small businesses use or build are just enough for what they need now. It's like building a walkway one step behind the person walking ahead of you. You're just playing catch-up.

The better way is to build systems for your business from the perspective of creating the capacity that you want to fill. You could say personal development is a system of developing yourself so that you can receive more. Now let's consider some business systems you might expect, but also some you may not, that are specifically applicable to self-employed business owners.

Strive to Be Bored

It's unlikely you'll ever hear an employer tell an employee to strive to be bored. But this works for us self-employed. The idea is to create downtime by getting rid of everything that's taking up time that isn't productive. My favorite book about time management is *Procrastinate on Purpose* by Rory Vaden for its simple step-by-step process to make time for yourself. Rory suggests these five pretty self-explanatory steps:

1. **Eliminate:** Yup, get rid of whatever you can to create time to be bored.

2. **Automate:** Use technology or habits to be efficient and gain time back.

3. **Delegate:** Seriously, you don't have to do everything yourself. Focus on what you do best.

4. **Procrastinate:** What can you put off that isn't important right now? Get rid of distractions.

5. **Concentrate:** What is your time best spent on right now? This is how you grow.

Once you've taken all these steps, you will likely find yourself with time on your hands. Our goal here is to strive to be bored! At the core of it, it's also the principle of LINGO and working only with your ideal customers. Too many businesses waste way too much time trying to satisfy customers who will never be satisfied. Non-ideal customers take up space, energy, and time. Boredom creates the capacity to be filled with far greater things, such as clients and tasks that will result in true business growth. When that capacity gets filled up, you trim again to create more capacity. And so on.

Maybe you've noticed this too, but there's almost always a correlation between making the most amount of money and working the least hard. On the contrary, when I'm busting my butt, there isn't as much coming in. Now, this may not be true in a seasonal business, but even still, the engine drives faster and smoother when all cylinders are firing.

So, you need to create a system for yourself to strive to be bored. Maybe you use Rory's system as a framework. Maybe you have your own process. Whatever it takes, get rid of time sucks, find yourself bored, and watch the value of your time increase. Once filled up, it's your choice whether you want to make room once again for additional growth. This is how you encourage and control your business growth.

Whereas the first system—strive to be bored—is about creating time and space, this next system is about making room for a greater volume of customers. Obviously, that will make your business grow! You can look at this as a blend of goal setting and manifestation. It's being aware of what you financially want, the goals you set, and how much space is available.

Make Space

Initially, my photography business was very seasonal. We would do 60 to 70 percent of annual sales in just four months—September through November. Being in the northeast, the beautiful fall colors were a motivator to do outdoor on-location portraits; plus, the session would double and triple up as gifts and holiday cards. Since it was a seasonal business, there was a lot of pressure to make sure we met our numbers in order to meet the goals for the year—not to mention the stockpile of cash flow that was needed to make it through the months when there was virtually no income. I used to say I was a modern-day farmer and the crop was cash. Plus, I'd have to maintain employee salaries and my own life during the slow months.

So, every year prior to September 1, I'd do a calculation to understand how many photo shoots we would need to do in those four months. I'd subtract year-to-date sales from the annual sales goal, and voila, I'd have a sales goal we had to meet in the four remaining months. I'd know the average sale we were running for the year, so I'd divide the remaining sales goals by the average sale. This would result in a total number of clients needed to meet the financial goals. I say *financial* goals because it was more than a sales goal, as it may be for you as well. It was about the financial need to pay my bills, support my staff, live my life, maybe save for the future, and have the cash flow needed to keep going. Those are living goals. So much more than sales goals, because this shit is real.

This is when the idea of making space gets fun. With a known number of clients needed for the remainder of the year, the first thing to do was confirm we had the time capacity to meet that goal. If you can't, refer to "Strive to Be Bored" above. You may have choices that need to be made. Maybe additional hours are needed. Perhaps more staff. You might consider other ways to be more efficient. You know how much capacity you need to accommodate the number of customers you want. If there isn't enough capacity, you can either make space or lower your goals. Your choice. But now you're in control of outcomes.

Now, I'm a visual person. Perhaps you are too. A powerful tool to concentrate and manifest the number of customers you need is to create some sort of visual of your volume goal. In my photography business, we would have a white board with a stroke mark representing each client we needed. If we needed forty clients to book, there would be forty stroke marks. As a session was booked, we erased a stroke mark. To track speaking gigs, I set aside the number of books for the number of

Build systems for your business from the perspective of creating the capacity that you want to fill.

---

speaking gigs I want to do. I send one to each meeting planner. For branding and coaching clients today, I have a spreadsheet with a column for each service I provide. Down each column is a 1. The spreadsheet tallies up at the bottom of the column. When I gain a new client, I remove a 1 from the top so the tally decreases at the bottom.

I'm a believer in seeing what you want as a form of manifestation. That's why these visuals work. You also want to start with visuals that represent your maximum capacity. It's energetically a lot more powerful to see yourself at maximum capacity first and then reduce the need as you go along. This way, you are believing in your maximum capacity and getting excited as you see yourself getting closer and closer to your goal.

Counting down is also a known method of retention. If you tell someone you're going to give them ten tips and start with number one, ten can feel like a long way to go. Whereas if you count backward, from ten to one, there's great anticipation as you head toward number one. By starting with whatever number represents full capacity and then subtracting, you create a similar high level of anticipation and excitement toward the end goal.

Benefits and Perks

You know those benefits and perks that come with having a traditional job, like paid vacations, sick days, and summer Fridays? Maybe some technology and training? When's the last time you treated yourself as a self-employed business owner to any of those things? Never? Why not?

More than likely, it just never occurred to you. It's time to change that. Be your own Head of People, as they say at Google, and design your own system of benefits and perks. How many weeks' vacation time will you get per year? *Paid* vacation, that is! How many personal days are you going to allow yourself without guilt? Don't you miss the sudden surprise of a snow day? Make your own snow days or personal days and allow yourself a few days a year for spontaneity without guilt. Guess what? The business will go on. What about summer Fridays?

I admit, sometime in June, I often start getting jealous as I see people posting on social media that they got out early on Fridays or didn't work at all. After thirty-five years in business, I decided to create that for myself. My work week ends at noon on Fridays for July and August. It's amazing how much better I felt I was treating myself when I started this! You know the phrase, "My boss is a jerk and I'm self-employed"? Well, he's not such a jerk anymore. I quite like the guy for giving me Friday afternoons off during the summer. Besides, it's hot in Miami then, so some extra pool or beach time is a big plus.

Like your own personal HR department, Head of People, or other voice in your head, sit down and build the system for the benefits and perks you deserve at the beginning of the year. Or heck, do it now at whatever point of the year. The point is to do it. You deserve the same and more benefits and perks people get in traditional jobs. This is how you control your schedule.

Having set yourself up on all these systems to do more and enjoy more, let's switch gears to the practical side of systems.

Technology That Grows with You

One of the biggest problems I see small businesses create for themselves is that they make choices about systems and technology based on current needs rather than future needs. Thinking about capacity, you want to make your technology choices based on the business to come. Your future capacity.

A perfect example is customer relationship management (CRM). Good CRM technology can be expensive. But before you go too cheap, think about future capacity. I've seen many entrepreneurs choose a CRM solution that is limited to a small number of emails in a database. A maximum of one thousand email addresses might sound great now, when you're starting out with your list of twenty-five. But using Hug Marketing techniques, it won't be long before you hit one thousand emails in your database. Then what? Unless your choice of CRM offers a larger plan, you're kind of screwed. It's not so easy to migrate your list. It's even questionable whether you're allowed to by FCC regulations. I know business owners who had to ask their list of customers to opt in again to the new system and lost nearly 50 percent of their list, those who didn't bother or want to.

The ideal technologies to choose are those that grow as your business grows. Maybe they have a step-up plan with an increase in subscription. Whether it's CRM tech, website hosting, workflow, bookkeeping, invoicing, podcast recording, or numerous other tasks in your business, choose the technology that allows for your increased capacity with a minimum amount of hassle. Be convinced you're going to grow. Free or low cost can seem appealing, but it's not a good option if it's going to limit your capacity. Cost and user friendliness are certainly important considerations when choosing technology for your business, but not nearly as important as choosing for your future capacity.

Build a Support System

Those who support you and your business are not often thought of as a system, but they are also part of it. Whether they are employees, virtual assistants, coaches, mentors, peers, or consultants, they play a vital role in the ecosystem of your business. As an old African proverb states, "If you want to go fast, go alone. If you want to go far, go together." I'm willing to bet that you're in this for the long haul. You want to go far. Support yourself and your business by surrounding yourself with a great team and what I refer to as a band of angels. My band of angels are those individuals in my business life, some close, many not so close, who just seem to show up when I need them. Maybe they refer a client. Or drop a great idea when you need it. The key to a great team is to think of it as a vital part of a healthy system. Healthy for you and for everyone in it.

As business owners who take things personally, we can often be controlling because, hey, it's our reputation on the line. But being controlling of someone or not delegating because you want control over the outcome is misdirected control. To get the best results, take control over hiring or collaborating only with the best people. Then trust what you saw in them when you hired them and leave them alone to do their thing. In the end, your entire business is enriched because of the trust you put in others. This is how you control quality.

It's worth reiterating here that you went into business to control your destiny and found yourself in uncontrollable circumstances. The goal of the Self-Employed Ecosystem is to show you a way to set up far more control of your results than you may ever have imagined. Setting up systems is part of that. In doing so, you gain the ability to control your growth, outcomes, schedule, and quality. That's powerful!

With effective systems opening up doors for you to grow your business and welcome in more customers, now let's look at how to keep those customers. In Hug Marketing, this is the ultimate goal—when they aren't just regular customers, but loyal customers and advocates.

9

Develop Loyalty, Advocates, and Referrals

MATTHEW, A photographer, was a student in a six-month photography business program I offered for many years. He mentioned that he hadn't sent out a promotional email to his client list in eight years. Eight years! My only response was, "Wait... what? How is that even possible?" Several of the other students in the group of twelve admitted they hadn't emailed their clients in years either. Mind you, these are all business owners in an educational business program because they need their business to do better.

"So, what then?" I asked. "You're all just doing one-offs?"

That was pretty much the case: they sat around waiting for that lucky opportunity when a past client thought to contact them. Talk about working harder than you have to! Talk about not having control of your business!

The easiest way to new business for you is through past clients who were happy with what you provided. To not maintain your relationships with them is literally leaving money on the table.

Right away, Matthew and I got busy crafting his email blast to his past clients. That one mailing brought in eight portrait sessions. With an average of three to four thousand dollars per session, he brought in some serious money. Cost? Zero.

A Meaningful and Monetarily Smart Strategy

That experience with Matthew was when I started realizing how many businesses leave money on the table, opportunities unrealized, and relationships unnurtured by not thinking about customer loyalty and retention. If ever there was a maintenance system to keep your business healthy, it's increasing retention and customer loyalty. Customer loyalty is your gold mine. Not nurturing customer loyalty is not only a crime toward your business, but also potentially unkind.

Years ago, as I built my database of emails, I carefully tagged my friends and family to exclude them from my promotional emails and newsletter. They were on my list because maybe they bought my book or opted into something to show their support. But they're my friends and family. Let's face it: they're never going to hire me and it's kind of embarrassing to show up acting all professional in front of those closest to you.

One day, I had a revelation. Cue heavenly music from above. Seriously, it was a big moment of awareness for me. I realized that I would probably behave differently if I knew my family and friends were on my email list. And if I want those on my list, clients and prospective clients, to get to know me better, the authentic me, shouldn't I show up for them the same way I do for family and friends? If I want to earn their hug, shouldn't I treat them like family and friends? Of course, I should! And so should you.

I added my family and friends back on my email list. From that point forward, they would receive my emails and newsletter just like everyone else on the list. If you did the same, would it affect what you send out and how often?

If you craft and design the email you're sending out with your friends and family in mind, you are more likely to speak authentically, in a way they would feel is the real you. For some reason, when business owners put on their marketing hats, they become some other version of themselves that isn't as genuine. Maybe it's a professional facade, or the way they think they're supposed to look and sound for a particular industry. But when you know you're speaking to your friends, you break through that facade barrier. When you don't, you may feel a little awkward in front of your friends and family.

It also helps you to know how frequently to email. If you keep your friends and family in mind, you'll know when you're sending out emails too often and when it feels annoying. Besides, your friends and family will be the first to let you know. The bigger problem for many businesses, though, is usually not emailing often enough. Like Matthew. Can you imagine not being in touch with family and friends for eight years? Yes, it would be unkind! Having your friends and family on your email list can shift your thinking from waiting for "love 'em and leave 'em" one-off clients to nurturing and building relationships.

This is the goal of Hug Marketing. The final frontier and innermost circle: when customers become repeat customers, advocates, and sources of referrals. There is nothing more meaningful and monetarily smart for your business. As is often said in business, it costs a fraction of the amount of money to keep a past customer than it does to acquire a new one. It often requires almost no investment except time and care.

In my photography business, we always maintained a 60 to 70 percent repeat customer rate. It was the first metric we would review at the end of the year. That one metric tells you a lot. If a previously healthy repeat customer rate starts to go down, there are bigger issues in your business, because keeping customers who were previously happy should be the easiest thing to do. Maybe quality is slipping. Perhaps service isn't what they are used to. Or, as is often the case, you're not paying attention to them.

This metric also lets you know how much new business you need to meet your goals. If your typical repeat customer rate is 50 percent, or even 20 percent, that lets you know that you need enough marketing efforts for only 50 percent or 80 percent of your total business goals. Whatever the starting point is, at least by knowing how much repeat business you can expect, you're not starting from zero. And if you see it starting to slip, you can look at the areas in your business that may need some work.

Let's look at some strategies to increase your customer repeat business as well as turn customers into advocates.

Presumptive Language

From day one of working with a new customer, speak to them as if they are going to be a forever customer. You can say things like, "Next time you order..." or, "In the future..." As my friend Brant Menswar, author of *Black Sheep*, says, speak it into existence. If you genuinely feel as if you have just connected with someone you want to have a long-term relationship with, speak to them as such. It's not going to sound salesy when it comes from a genuine place; it will sound committed to doing such a great job for them and providing such an amazing experience that you're confident they'll want to call you again. Presumptive language, when it comes from a place of authenticity, lets your customer know you intend on building a relationship by always doing right by them.

**Customer loyalty
is your gold mine**. Not nurturing
customer loyalty
is not only a
crime toward your
business, but
also potentially
unkind.

When a new client committed to an upcoming portrait session in my photography business, I often arranged a visit to their home, usually to get some ideas on locations to photograph as well as to help the client prepare clothing and so on. I also suggested we walk around the home together to consider places they might hang their beautiful portraits. I would intentionally look for the hallway outside bedrooms or the empty walls going up stairs and suggest those might be great places to build a wall of portraits. I asked, "How do you envision this being decorated with portraits over the next ten years?" Do you see what I did there?

Presumption No. 1: They are going to buy portraits to hang on the wall and not just eight-by-ten-inch photos for a mantel or table.

Presumption No. 2: We're going to work together for the next ten years.

Use presumptive language to set up the sale you want, that allows you to do what you're best at and that you feel is the most satisfying work to do. Frankly, you shouldn't have any products or services in your business that don't allow you to do your best and that you don't enjoy doing. Always use presumptive language to set up a loyal and ongoing relationship.

Review the conversations you have with first inquiries, sales conversations, and become highly conscious of all interactions with your customers to see where you can speak in terms of "when" instead of "hope to see you again sometime, maybe."

Create a Product Suite

Another way to retain your customers is with a product suite mentality. Apple, of course, is the master of the product suite. The devices are so interconnected, people joke that it's like belonging to a cult; that once you buy one, it's all "downhill" from there. Apple is the potato chip of business: you can't have just one. Yes, it can be annoying, but without a doubt, the relationship between the products encourages you to buy more. I think AirDrop alone may keep me a loyal customer for life. The ability to move content so easily from one device to another is everything to me.

You can also capture the essence of a product suite by having highly customizable parts of your business that are not easily duplicated. In my photography business, all the frames for the wall portraits were custom made by hand in unique finishes. My clients would not be able to acquire these frames elsewhere. Many were even my own design and finish combinations. Knowing I had clientele so particular that they would never add frames that didn't match or a different style of photography, I offered items that kept them wanting to come back.

Services can also be made into a product suite if you have a step-up or step-down model. In fact, I suggest having both. Typically, businesses have a step-up model. A customer enters at one level and is given the opportunity to step up to a higher, more expensive level (the upsell). That works! Better still is a step-up and step-down model with the possibility of various peaks.

For example, I enter into a relationship with most of my clients at a moderate investment level, most often through my Small Business Branding or Small Business Consulting programs. Often, they see me at a speaking event, read my books, or hear me on a podcast. These are one-to-one coaching programs for two to three months respectively at a fixed rate. In these programs, we do amazing work and the client receives excellent value. Once completed, they have an option to step up to longer-term one-to-one coaching or step down to the Self-Employed Life Group that supports them moving forward.

Because the relationship continues, a client in our coaching group can step up to one-to-one at any time, and likewise, my one-to-one clients can step down to the Self-Employed Life Group to create a support system for themselves. The point is, there's always a place to go and stay in a relationship together. Of course, there's always the option to not take any step right away. Some clients come back later, but rarely do I not continue some sort of active relationship with a client. They are simply moving up and down a scale. That's a product suite that creates a step-up, step-down business model based on your Business Model of Multiples.

Step-Up/Step-Down Business Model

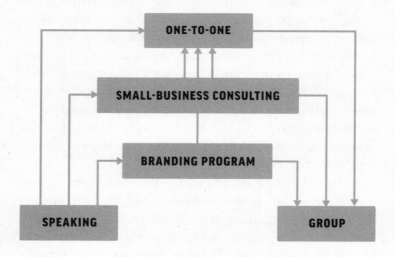

In your business, consider where you can offer highly customizable products and services that your clients cannot get elsewhere. Look for opportunities for your products or services to be linked together so that having one makes a customer want to have another. Lastly, have a range of products and services that allow customers to move up and down a scale but never leave the nest. That will keep your customers loyal.

Favor Existing Customers

How many times have you seen businesses promote a deal for new customers only? I have to say, this has to be one of my biggest pet peeves. What could be more harmful to a relationship than ignoring the fact that someone has done business with you, and showing privilege to a new customer? Drives me insane! We self-employed and small-business owners are very relationship-based—relationally reliant, for that matter. We count on repeat business, and I'm pretty sure you've got the point by now that you can probably do better. Why on earth would a business show favor to a new customer? Imagine me shaking my head.

Let's flip the script. In my opinion, there should be an established program within every small business that shows favor to existing customers, whether there's a price incentive when sliding up and down the scale of services or added benefits for being an ongoing customer. In my photography business, we had one of the most powerful customer incentive programs I know of.

One of the biggest growing pains I faced in my photography business was that for several years, I had an eight-week waiting list. Being the only photographer, I had only so much time available. My rates were high enough, but even still, the demand was greater than the capacity. The worst part was that my earlier clients, those who supported me as an up-and-coming photographer, stood to suffer the worst. Prior to this time crunch, they were used to getting a session booked in a week or two. Now we were telling them they had to wait eight weeks! This was not going over well. I feared losing a lot of customers, so I had to come up with a solution. But honestly, more than anything, it felt wrong. It's not who I am.

So, we designed a priority client pre-pay offer. Each year in February, past clients were given the opportunity to pre-pay for a session for any time later that year. Yes, it offered them a discount, but the main benefit to the client was that it would guarantee that we would set up their session ten weeks before their desired time frame. We kept our best clients ahead of the eight-week waiting list. Problem solved, and we maintained our 60 to 70 percent repeat client rate. Today I work only with those photography clients who pre-pay, so that I can control the limited number of sessions I do each year and no longer accept new clients.

What past-customer-only incentive programs can you create? This is a great way to express your gratitude for their support of your business and to build an ongoing relationship. In fact, I think it's the best and most respectful way. Every business should have a benefit and an incentive for a customer to become a repeat customer. How else are you going to get them in the innermost circle of the Hug Marketing diagram?

Be Frictionless

For people today, one of the things with the greatest value is time. None of us has enough time. As a business, if you can give time back to your customers, they will love you for it and keep coming back. Ask yourself this question: Do your customers prioritize money over time or time over money? Be honest and objective asking yourself this question. Almost always, the answer is that your customers value their time over money. If they didn't, there wouldn't be such things as rush charges, guaranteed delivery, or FedEx, for that matter. Yet, businesses often behave as if their customers value money over time.

Today, the best way to save your customers' time is to make doing business with you as frictionless as possible. As consumers, we are being trained to value frictionless business. It's why we love ride-share and food delivery apps—they're convenient, on our phone, we don't have to call, we see all our choices, and payment is easy with our credit card already built in. I, for one, crave a frictionless experience and am always looking for businesses to make my life easier. I'm a big fan of TaskRabbit for getting work done around my home and Rover for dogsitting. I order almost everything online and use Apple Pay as often as possible. My phone is always with me. My wallet may not be.

To find out just how frictionless of an experience your customer wants, ask them what their preferred method of communication is. On the one hand, if they say, "Call me and leave a voicemail/message on my answering machine," well then, you have a customer who likes things the old-fashioned way. But be forewarned, they may drive you crazy because they likely have time on their hands. On the other hand, the customer who wants you to interact via email or even text is used to technology, has a lot going on, and wants as frictionless an experience as possible.

Review every touch point in your business to consider how you can make it more frictionless. Maybe you can use an online booking option, FAQs, helpful videos, an app, a quick response team, live chat, online payment, or resources easily accessible online. The list of opportunities to be frictionless is almost unlimited. Let's be clear: frictionless is not less personal. In fact, I'd say it's the other way around. Giving customers back time by creating a frictionless experience shows respect for their lives, and I like to think that the time saved enables them to spend more time doing what they love to do and being with those they love. It shows great care for them, exceptional service, and a commitment to a long-lasting relationship.

It costs a fraction of the amount of money to keep a past customer than it does to acquire a new one.

Inspire Referrals

The other thing you are striving for in the center of Hug Marketing is to turn your customers into advocates of your brand and sources of referrals. However, most businesses do this wrong.

I have asked thousands of attendees at speaking events what motivates them to refer a business. Everyone has the same answer: to help out a friend. When I ask what's most important to them in referring the friend, everyone also says, "That my friend also has a great experience." Think about it. Is that true for you? If you refer a friend to, say, a hair salon, don't you hope they have as good an experience as you had? I mean, you don't seriously hope they get their hair botched. Remember, I qualified this by saying it was a friend. What do you hope to get in return? Most people say they don't want anything—maybe just acknowledgment of appreciation from the business owner. Over the years, no one has said that getting paid for the referral is what inspired them to give the referral. OK, one person did. Everyone else, thousands, said what mattered most was that their friend also had a great experience.

Why, then, do businesses try to inspire referrals with the offer of a discount? A simple thank-you and acknowledgment from the business goes much further than money ever will.

The other reason many businesses don't get the referrals they would like is that they ask at the wrong time. Almost every business waits until the service has been provided or the product is purchased to ask for the referral. That can work, especially if it's a quick transaction or purchase. But often there are better times.

Let's look at why waiting until the end may not work. For one, if it's a higher-end purchase, they may have spent more money than they intended. They're hopefully glad they made the purchase, but it stings a bit at the moment. Not to worry. We all know the sting wears off. But is it the right time to ask for referrals? Probably not.

The purchase may also be something they got off their checklist and you are simply not top of mind anymore. When you ask for referrals, they will politely nod with the best of intentions and then forget.

Often, the end of a working relationship is transactional, so customers are not really in an emotional state. It's why I always have all my services paid for prior to completion. I don't like to mix the joy of what we created together, be it a collection of portraits or a newly branded website, with a financial transaction.

With this in mind, look for other opportunities in your process to ask for referrals. In my photography business, I used to ask at the end of the photo shoot. There was no time they were ever going to be happier with me! The session had just gone better than they expected, I masterfully convinced their kids to have a good time, and they hadn't spent a substantial amount of money yet!

Have you ever had a brand-new client refer you before you even started working together? I'll bet you have! They are so excited about finding you or the prospect of what you offer, they may be more eager than at any other time to tell other people. Encourage it! With such a great connection, mention that you would love to find more customers just like them!

With these ideas, you can turn your customers into repeat clients, advocates, and sources of referrals. You will have made it all the way to the final destination of marketing—the hug. What could be better? This truly is the sweet spot of business— when a percentage of your business comes from repeat customers and they are spreading the word about you. You grow exponentially by constantly adding new customers to the group hug. These are the customers you would literally hug given the opportunity.

10

Spread the Word
with Podcasts

HAVING BEEN a podcast host for over six years and broadcasted more than six hundred episodes at the time of writing, it would seem a bit irresponsible of me to not offer you some tips on how to use podcasts to market your business. Podcasting is one of the fastest-growing media channels there is, which offers a tremendous opportunity. But I have high standards when it comes to hosting and being a guest on podcasts. As with any other art form, I respect it for what it is and believe we should always strive to uphold a high standard of quality, integrity, and legacy.

You may not think of being a guest on a podcast as a system, but if you want to be effective and efficient at it, trust me, you'll want to create a system. There's knowing what podcasts to reach out to; the pitch you have to create in advance; listening to the show ahead of time; providing content, information, your bio, and a headshot for the host; being prepared for the interview; having a lead magnet to give away; and maybe owning a domain that redirects to your lead magnet. Being ready to share the episode once it's broadcast is also important. There are so many steps, you must have a system.

Should You Have Your Own Podcast?

Let's get the first question out of the way. Should you have your own podcast? Truthfully, I do everything I can to discourage people from starting their own podcast. First of all, it's either a lot of time or a lot of money. To think that it's not going to cost you either way is naive.

When I launched *Creative Warriors* in July 2014, we boot-strapped the podcast for the first two years. We had no idea what we were doing and had no prior audio editing experience, but we managed to do all the production in-house. It was very time-consuming. But like a lot of self-employed business owners, we do what we have to do in the beginning. We didn't have an audience large enough to be appealing to a sponsor, so it was either do it ourselves or dish out a lot of money. Without justification to spend the money, we did it all in-house.

I was fortunate when I launched; I had a fairly decent email list. Our first month, we had about fourteen hundred downloads. It gradually grew and we seemed to hang at around twenty-five hundred downloads a month for about eighteen months. Then, all of a sudden, something clicked. The audience grew, we appeared on a couple of "best of" lists, and we got better at what we do. The show shot up to ten thousand downloads a month, so that two years in, we were able to afford a full production team. Since then, all I have to do is read every book and prep for the interviews, and my podcast team does all production post-interview.

It took two years to get to the point of being able to hire a production company. So, it's either a lot of time or a lot of money, which is why, at last check, the average podcast lasts only about seven episodes. That's when people wake up to this reality and give up. This is why I discourage people from starting their own show—to protect them from the illusion that it's easy and to avoid inundating the market so much that standards get lower. Also, if I discourage someone from starting their own podcast and they are committed to doing it anyway, they are far more likely to stick it out and produce a great show. There's always room for more great content.

Honestly, though, for many business owners, being a great guest is a better way to go. You can gain incredible exposure without having to produce your own show and without the hassle or expense.

Hosting my show and chatting with amazing guests is one of the greatest pleasures of my day. Also, without a doubt, it has elevated my brand and name recognition beyond what I could have hoped for. And the best part is the amazing relationships that have been formed with guests and listeners. As I travel for business and speaking, I often meet up with a fan of the show, and hardly anything is more satisfying. (Not to mention the number of people who come up to me at speaking gigs and know far more about me than I'm even comfortable with. I do overshare a bit on the show.) So, don't get me wrong. Hosting a podcast is an honor and incredibly rewarding. But you can definitely spread the word about your business by being an awesome guest. That's what we're going to focus on.

Find Your Value

Is being a guest on a podcast a great way to market any business? Maybe not every type of business, but I'm pretty hard-pressed to think of one that can't benefit. There is literally a show out there for every topic imaginable. The key is to find the value in what you do for others so that it doesn't feel like you're marketing at all, either to the audience or the host. If it feels to me like someone wants to be a guest on our show to "market" themselves, it's a no-go. In fact, there have been times when I felt a guest had a genuine desire to offer terrific content, but also like they had something to sell, which made it hard to choose them. For example, I really felt that Ethan Beute, chief evangelist at video technology company BombBomb.com, had a lot to offer on the topic of making emails more personable. The challenge was how to angle the conversation toward great lessons for the audience without pitching the product. So, we chose the route of talking about how videos in email can rehumanize your interactions with your customers in a way that regular email cannot. Sure, this is exactly what BombBomb does. But the mission was a clean one: to help business owners connect more deeply with their customers, which is foundational to what our show is all about. So, we were able to make it work without feeling like it was marketing the product.

That will be the key for you as well—finding the value in your message that transcends what you do or have to offer. Interviewing authors is easy because while their goal is to promote their book, it's full of rich content that makes for a great conversation and changes the lives of listeners. Everyone knows the author guest wants to promote their book, but as long as there's value in the content, everyone wins.

What you have to offer, be it a book, service, or product, has to become desirable to the listening audience only after you have provided great value in the content. Otherwise, it's just a pitch, and who wants to listen to a podcast that's nothing more than a pitch?

Can you find the substantive value in what you do that will make listeners want what you offer without you needing to blatantly promote it? For example, let's say you're a chef with various products such as online cooking classes, a course, and

Find the substantive value in what you do

that will make listeners want what you offer without you needing to blatantly promote it.

---

home-delivery meals. Perhaps your area of expertise is plant-based foods. The most obvious shows on which to share your value would be those geared toward nutrition and healthy eating. You could talk about the principles and benefits of a plant-based lifestyle. You can imagine this would generate interest in your products. You could be on a show about entrepreneurial journeys and share the story of how you built your business. Since you have an online course or two, you could be on a podcast sharing ideas on developing and marketing an online business. Perhaps you could be on a lifestyle show and talk about time management and how home delivery of meals is aligned with today's busy lifestyle. You could even be on shows that are environmentally conscious and talk about how plant-based eating is better for the environment. I could go on and on. While your core topic is plant-based eating and nutrition, as you can see, there are several genres of shows on which you could be a guest, add value to the listeners, and indirectly promote your business. You're giving value first and marketing your business second.

As I said, I'm hard-pressed to think of any business that doesn't have one or more topics that wouldn't be fascinating content while promoting services or products along the way. If you are a locally based business, there may be a show specific to your area. If your service is bound by a region, being on a national or international podcast can appear prestigious to your audience and worthy of publicity. It can elevate your local business to a new status.

Find the Right Podcasts

Now you have to find the shows to be on. As it turns out, this is one of the biggest challenges because podcasts are ubiquitous. So, first, know the genre. Are you looking to be on shows about entrepreneurship, baking, traveling, personal development, technology, or writing pens? No matter how obscure your topic is, there's likely a podcast out there for it. You just need to narrow the field.

The search field in iTunes and other podcast apps works a lot like a Google search. While most people search for a particular show or host by name, you can also search by topic. That's likely to still provide too many choices. Narrow it down further.

First, be sure the show is active by looking at the last episode broadcast. If the show hasn't broadcasted recently or on a regular basis, don't bother. Keep in mind: podcasts are evergreen, so shows that are dead are still going to be listed.

Second, be sure they have guests! Many podcasts don't. Nothing is more embarrassing than reaching out to be a guest on a show that doesn't host them. I've made that mistake. Whoops.

Next, narrow down your options further to be sure the show has an audience size worthy of your time. You'll never know for sure how many downloads a show receives each month or how many subscribers or followers they have. However, you can tell a bit by the number of reviews. If they have just a few reviews, the show isn't generating enough interest. I like to see a couple dozen reviews at least. Don't get me wrong, I am often a guest on a brand-new show. But when I do that, it's because I want to support the host and the idea of a great new podcast in the world. But if your objective is reaching people to expand your business, you need a show with a substantial audience. Checking out how many reviews a podcast has will at least show how much effort the host is putting into growing their show and how engaged their audience is, as well as provide at least an idea of the audience size.

By taking these steps—knowing the genre, making sure the show is active and has guests, and has an audience size worthy of your time—you will have narrowed your options (don't worry: with the number of podcasts out there, you'll have more than enough to pick from even after this), and now you also have the comfort of knowing it will be worth your time. As a busy self-employed business owner, you don't have time and energy to waste.

Craft Your Pitch

Now, it's time to pitch to the host or their producers. Keep in mind, the host may get several or dozens of inquiries a day from people wanting to be on their show. Be respectful of their time. Very few podcast hosts earn a living from their podcast. That means podcasting is part of the bigger picture of their business, which is why you need to be concise and exceptional in order to stand out and get their attention quickly.

Here's how to be exceptional when pitching a host: Send a very brief email or note through a contact form. Know something about the show and audience, immediately describe your topic, explain what makes you unique, and tell them what the audience is going to gain. It's that simple.

However, doing that in a short and concise email is not simple. Do not BS. If you don't know anything about the show, educate yourself first. But do not tell them you're a big fan of the show and then pitch your idea of home decorating to a true crime show. Booking agencies are the worst at this! They make no connection between the topic and the show and just blitzkrieg podcasts looking to place their client. Don't be like a booking agency. Don't waste everyone's time.

Here's an example of an excellent pitch to be on my podcast:

My awesome boss, Kasey Compton, is on a mission to help self-employed and small-business owners find their entrepreneurial confidence. The problem is, entrepreneurs often try to build up confidence within themselves with "fake it till you make it" attitudes and power stances.

It turns out, a large part of entrepreneurial confidence comes from having confidence in their systems. As a licensed therapist with an expertise in anxiety and panic disorders, Kasey brings a unique perspective on the topic of confidence in systems. You see, the root of panic disorders is when someone's logical mind is disconnected from their body system. The same is true with business owners. When they don't have confidence in their business systems, it breaks down their confidence. Anxiety and panic can ensue.

Kasey is eager to bring clarity on these topics to your audience of self-employed business owners:

- *How to determine the systems they need*
- *Ways to prioritize their to-do list*
- *Systems to create a business that runs without them*
- *Creating consistent customer service as a system*
- *What to do when their business feels like a toddler*
- *Connecting their mindset to their systems to gain entrepreneurial confidence*

If you agree Kasey would bring value to your audience, please let me know the next steps.

Thank you and have a terrific day!
Erin Norstrand

Let's break down this pitch so you can see why it works and how you can follow this format.

My awesome boss, Kasey Compton...
Starts off casual, friendly, and light. Lets me know the sender is speaking on behalf of her boss. The email can come from you, too, but there is an impression of you being a bigger deal when someone else sends it. However, if someone sends

the email on your behalf, they should not give a lengthy explanation of who they are, what they do, and their position.

>   *...is on a mission to help self-employed and small-business
>   owners find their entrepreneurial confidence.*

Boom! Lets me know that they know my show because she's
called out self-employed and small-business owners, and it's
not an email blast. Let's me know she's not just "calling it in,"
because I don't want a guest to show up like that.

>   *The problem is entrepreneurs often try to build up confidence
>   within themselves with "fake it till you make it" attitudes and
>   power stances.*

Gets my attention because she's stating the problem and
backing it up with common knowledge. She has my attention
because I agree.

>   *It turns out, a large part of entrepreneurial confidence comes
>   from having confidence in their systems.*

She's got my attention also because she's saying something
a bit disruptive and is stating what the topic of conversation
will be.

>   *As a licensed therapist with an expertise in anxiety and panic
>   disorders, Kasey brings a unique perspective on the topic of con-
>   fidence in systems. You see, the root of panic disorders is when
>   someone's logical mind is disconnected from their body system.
>   The same is true with business owners. When they don't have con-
>   fidence in their business systems, it breaks down their confidence.
>   Anxiety and panic can ensue.*

Brilliant! This is everything because now she's stated why
Kasey is different. This is her unique perspective. A host may
get several emails a week from experts who want to talk about

improving systems in one form or another. But how many do you think are coming from a therapist who specializes in panic disorders and makes the connection between anxiety, panic, and business systems? ONE!

Kasey is eager to bring clarity on these topics to your audience of self-employed business owners:
* *How to determine the systems they need*
* *Ways to prioritize their to-do list*
* *Systems to create a business that runs without them*
* *Creating consistent customer service as a system*
* *What to do when their business feels like a toddler*
* *Connecting their mindset to their systems to gain entrepreneurial confidence*

Provides several specific topics to talk about. We can go deep on one or two or touch on all of them. Aim to offer enough choices but not too many—five to seven is fine.

If you agree Kasey would bring value to your audience, please let me know the next steps.

Shows she understands about the audience and includes a call to action.

That's how you write a pitch! As a host, I look forward to receiving many more pitches like that. (I may have just done the world a great service by saving hosts tons of time and helping brilliant experts get the time in the spotlight they deserve!)

On another note, how big your own following is and your willingness to share the episode can help but are not more important than the value of the content you offer. It's only worth mentioning your social media following if you truly have influence. Don't be discouraged if you have no following at all, because truthfully, the majority of hosts care most about the

You can be an awesome podcast guest and gain **exposure for your business**.

———————————

content. It's actually pretty rare that the guests with the biggest names and followings are going to share the episode anyway. If your content is good and you're compelling, that's more important. You can include a one sheet or bio if you'd like, but providing links to other podcasts you've been on is rarely useful. Again, the host is short on time and likely won't listen to them.

Be an Awesome Guest

Now it's time to shine! You must have a good mic and a quiet place. There are many good mics and headsets to choose from. Do a little research. You also want good headphones so you don't get any feedback or bleed into your mic. The host has done a lot of work to build their show and audience. Social media is rented land; a podcast is owned media. Their name is affiliated with the show, and they want to maintain their reputation. Be prepared, professional, and prompt. Be sure there aren't background noises and all of your phone notifications are turned off.

There are nuances of podcasting that you want to be aware of. The only sense being activated by the listener is hearing. You want to be clear and concise in speaking. Listening to a podcast is also a passive activity, meaning very often the listener is doing something else at the same time, such as driving, walking, jogging, strolling with kids, or working. For that reason, you want to be prepared with some attention-getting comments or quotes and very memorable phrases. Think in terms of what will stand out and be memorable when they don't have the opportunity to write anything down. I highly recommend you think of these ahead of time and look for opportunities to drop them into the conversation. In fact, I even recommend having notes for yourself, perhaps taped to a wall because you don't want to risk the sound of shuffling papers coming over the mic. Yes, it's your content and you know your stuff, but your brain can go blank on a show. Create compelling and memorable sound bites to help the listeners retain your key points.

One of the most important things is to stay on message. You got on the show because of a great pitch. Now it's your job to deliver on that promise. Don't wander all over the place. And do yourself a favor and stay on-brand! Yes, you're on the show to provide value, but you're also on the show to serve your business.

Let's say your topic is about helping entrepreneurs get to their next level. Don't talk about that idea as growing your business, expanding your business, or elevating your business. Talk about taking your business to the next level and nothing else. It drives me crazy when my guests don't do this for themselves. I'm always bringing the conversation back around to their own topic. Stay on your own branded message and you'll be far more memorable.

Make it personal. A great and kind thing to do is call the host by name occasionally throughout the conversation. Do clarify with the host ahead of time what their preference is. Don't assume they want to be called by a nickname. Truth be told, outside of work, everyone calls me Jeff, as do many of my clients. I actually prefer Jeff. But for professional speaking and for SEO purposes, people know me as Jeffrey. So, it's always a little surprising to me when a guest calls me Jeff. It's not that I mind, but it feels inconsistent with my brand image, and I'm way too much of a neat freak for that. It's important to ask. If the show has a name for its community—I refer to my community as Warriors—referring to them as such will endear you with that community and the host, as well as make you part of the community. That's a wonderful thing to do to make it personal.

Lastly, with gratitude for the exposure of being a guest, you want to lead the audience to connect with you deeper. Try to lead listeners to someplace more engaging than your website.

Perhaps you have a gift to offer, a lead magnet, free content, or something that would be the beginning of a deeper relationship. Remember Hug Marketing? As podcast subscribers, they've moved into the "engaged" circle. You want to offer something exceptionally valuable to encourage them to take the next step and become connected with you. I'm a huge fan of having a memorable domain to lead to the content you are offering. Simply buy a catchy domain that reflects your offer and forward it to where it needs to go. For example, when I got accepted to do a TEDx Talk, I immediately purchased the domain JeffreyShawTedx.com, which just forwards to the video on the TED site. Imagine how much easier it is for the listener to hear a domain that they can remember and take action on later.

If you prepare to talk as if the listener can't write anything down, you are more likely to have memorable quotes ready, stay on message, and offer an easy-to-remember domain for them to connect deeper with you. Now you've been an awesome guest that served the host and their listeners, as well as your own business, by spreading the word about what you do to potentially thousands of people.

Conclusion: Business Strategies

This completes the all-important Business Strategies portion of the Self-Employed Ecosystem. You have gained so many business strategies that if you apply even a few, there's no way they can't dramatically improve your business. A quick review:

- Hug Marketing provides the path to enroll customers in a way that feels good.

- The Emotional Journey Website Map teaches you exactly how to lay out your website.

- The Business Model of Multiples can lead to greater control and multiple streams of income.

- Systems increase the capacity of what your business can handle.

- You can apply strategies to create loyal customers and inspire referrals.

- You can be an awesome podcast guest and gain exposure for your business.

By now you have probably realized that you have a lot more control than you may have originally thought. You have control of your personal development and how high you raise the ceiling of the success you are capable of achieving. You have control of moving people from being strangers to repeat customers with Hug Marketing. You now understand the power of priming to control the outcomes you want and to help people choose you. You have learned the emotional journey of your website to gain control over attracting your ideal customers. You've learned you can control the direction and income of your business by creating a Business Model of Multiples, whose levers you can adjust according to preference and need. You've seen how systems can provide control over the capacity your business can handle and open up the opportunity for growth. You've developed processes to control and increase customer loyalty so that you are always building on the business you already have. And you've even gained control of knowing how to market your business by being an awesome podcast guest.

Considering how out of control being self-employed can feel, you've just gained tremendous command of your destiny, don't you think? I am confident that when you apply even just these personal development and business strategies, you are going to see significant improvement in your business. No doubt. Like wrangling a wild herd of cattle, you are gaining control of your business.

All of that is well and good. In fact, I'd say it's downright awesome! If we left it right here, your effort up to this point would have been far worth it. In fact, in my experience, the most successful people I meet have mastered their personal development and taken action on many business strategies. Except for one thing. It likely won't stay that way without just a little more effort.

PART THREE

daily
habits

A S WE begin the Daily Habits portion of the Self-Employed Ecosystem, it's important to consider where you are at this point in developing and living in your ecosystem. The core challenge of being self-employed is that we want to gain control over our destiny without realizing perhaps just how uncontrollable the circumstances are. Check. Got it.

In my Small Business Consulting program, one of the first things I ask my clients to do is rate themselves, on a scale of 1 to 5, on how they are currently doing in all three areas of the Self-Employed Ecosystem: Personal Development, Business Strategies, and Daily Habits. Everyone always rates themselves lowest on daily habits. They are putting the least amount of effort into the very thing they know can even out the ups and downs of running their own business—what can help them create sustainable success and manage what they can't control. Believe me, I get it. Which is why I want to be realistic with you.

Can you expect to maintain your daily habits every day for all time? I know that's not realistic. But here's what I can tell you. The consistency of your daily habits is in direct proportion to the results you'll see. Especially when you apply all the personal development and business strategies you've learned and speed up the Growth Jet Lag (more on this later). The more consistent you are with your daily habits while incorporating change, the shorter the Growth Jet Lag and the sooner you'll get results. The more consistent you are with your daily habits, the less you will experience the roller coaster and the faster you'll recover from challenging times. These daily habits are not meant to be work or take up a lot of time. They are home base for you and should offer you respite from the crazy world of being self-employed. They offer all the support you deserve for being the awesome business warrior that you are.

11

Create a Steady Foundation

WHEN I hired my first business coach in 1999, our very first call changed my life and has everything to do with the roller coaster of business that we all experience. Mind you, my business was doing very well at this point. In fact, it was the beginning of many peak years to follow. But the truth is, I found it really lonely. I wanted someone to bounce ideas off of. I understood that how far I could go in business must be limited by what was in my own head and that the only way to go further was to collaborate with someone. For these reasons, I began my work with my first coach, Ron, whom I continued to work with for seven years. My experience of working with Ron was so impactful that I became a coach when he retired because I wanted to do for others what he did for me.

On our first coaching call, I mentioned to Ron that it seemed that one year my average sale would increase but the volume of sessions would be down. So, I'd work really hard at increasing the volume but then the next year, the average sale would be down. In my exact words, I said to Ron, "If I could ever get both right, it would be amazing." He said to me, "You know it's you that's causing it, right?"

Stop the Ups and Downs

That truth was life-changing for me, and I hope that simple bit of advice will be life-changing to you too. It's you who is causing the ups and downs. Well, maybe not *you* causing the ups and downs, because in all fairness, being self-employed often includes uncontrollable circumstances. But it *is* you who can stop it or at least create a steadier foundation.

I realized that I was doing what we all do: chasing what needed attention. Putting out fires. You put your attention on one thing, which means you're taking your eye off something else. I realized I had no practices and daily habits to create consistent and sustainable success. Without such habits, I would continue as many of us do, experiencing the highs and lows, the ups and downs, the running like a hamster on a wheel, riding the roller coaster, working really hard but hardly getting ahead.

That's when I began practicing yoga, studying Buddhism, meditating, and seeking out daily habits to not only keep my mind steady, but also achieve the goal to create steadiness and consistency in my business. Where a steady business exists, a consistent life follows, and vice versa.

What I learned after a deep dive into studying the inner workings of our souls is that there's a need for a happy medium if we want to apply new daily habits to our busy lives and businesses. The fact of the matter is, many practices such as yoga and meditation demand much effort and time and are rooted in an Eastern monastic lifestyle. That's great if you live in a monastery in Tibet. But we don't. (Or, I'm assuming not if you're reading this book!) We lead busy, multi-tiered lives. The happy medium is in taking these positive behaviors and realistically adapting them to and applying them in our everyday lives, the benefits of which will, in turn, spill over into our self-employed lives. When we do this, we truly have the opportunity for the best of both worlds, where East really meets West and the result is a steady inner environment prepared to manage the unsteady outer environment that we live in.

The personal development and business strategies I've shared really do help you gain control over seemingly uncontrollable circumstances. To create sustainable success, we must paradoxically step back into knowing that much of life is out of our control, but we can create steadiness by having the habits to see our way through. Now you're going to learn how to manage the natural ebbs and flows of any ecosystem, be it business or the ocean, without having to ride every wave.

When I started this book, someone asked me, "What's your new book about?" This was well before I even had an outline or title. It was mostly a concept. I said, "It's a book to help self-employed people learn to control what they can and how to manage what they can't."

The following habits will help you manage what you can't control in business and life. When practiced on a daily basis, they give you the ability to stay steady in the storm, otherwise known as self-employment, so that you have sustainable success.

Build Trust

The first of these daily habits is trust. Let's face it. It's so crazy being self-employed, we have to trust that there's a reason when it appears nothing is working out. And it can often feel that way. In a way, being independent-minded self-employed business owners has likely inadvertently trained us to *not* trust. Consider our very high level of care about what we do, our inclination toward perfectionism, often feeling like no one is going to do something as well as we can do it. We've put the weight of the world on our shoulders and unintentionally may have trained ourselves to trust only in ourselves. Or at least to a large part. The problem is, if you don't believe in something bigger than yourself, you're going to continue to put the weight of the world on your shoulders and you will be limited by how much you can carry.

However, trust is not passively waiting for things to work out or believing everything you want will come from manifestation. Trust is the active habit of believing—in yourself, in others; in what you gain, in what you lose. Believing in what you know. Believing in what you don't understand.

When you're a hard-working, self-employed business owner, there's nothing passive about trust. You have to pay your bills. You need to live. What I suggest is an active habit of trust to see you through the tough times. To keep you going. Trust that while timing may not be up to you, what you want to happen will happen. Trust that when one door closes, one or more doors open.

A habit of trust is beyond trusting others. It's trusting that there's more at play here than just you and your actions. It's trust in timing, in circumstances, and in what we don't know.

Your habit of trust can come in various forms, each one a personal choice. Perhaps you find trust in your faith. Maybe you see it more as a universal force or sense of spirituality. Regardless of where you place your trust, for that trust to be returned to you, it must become a habit. Perhaps it's prayer, meditation, or another form of ritual. But we all need a place to go, literally or figuratively, when we are challenged, which

Where a steady business exists, a consistent life follows, and vice versa.

you undoubtedly will be. For me, my trust habits are meditation and what I refer to as a trust mantra, which can be very useful.

A trust mantra is a phrase you can recite in your head when you need it—when you need to remind yourself that it's not all up to you, that you are protected in a cloak of trust, and somehow, someway, it will all work out. My trust mantra is: "When it looks like everything is falling apart, I trust that it's coming together for something bigger than I can imagine."

We may not understand. At times, we may not want what we're getting. Even still, we must trust. Because this crazy world of self-employment and uncontrollable circumstances is too hard otherwise. The way I look at it, what have you got to lose? How will you ever know you're wrong? Because if you keep on trusting, it's an infinite loop of possibility.

Trusting will also help you see things through. Have you ever seen the cartoon of the gold digger in a mine, picking away at the sides of a mineshaft? The cartoon strip progresses and the miner keeps chipping away, but eventually he gives up, drops his pick to the ground, and leaves. What we see next in the cartoon is that he was just inches from breaking through the wall when he quit, and on the other side is all the treasure he could imagine. The lesson, obviously, is that we never know how close we are to achieving our goal when we give up. So, we must keep going and trust in what might be on the other side of a challenge.

Many people were surprised to read in *LINGO* that I was rejected by twelve TEDx events before finally being accepted. I didn't give up. Do I think you should always just keep on going and going, perhaps chasing something that isn't a good idea in the first place? Or pursuing a business idea that isn't showing signs of working out, or, as Kevin O'Leary says on *Shark Tank*, that you should take it out back and shoot it? No, I don't. But if you know what trust feels like, you'll be able to distinguish whether an idea is worth pursuing because you trust it will work out. That's how I felt about TEDx. I trusted in not only knowing it would work out but also my ability to grow to meet the challenge. With trust, you'll also know when to walk away. Once you know the feeling of trust, you'll be able to accurately determine what's worthy of pursuing and what should be left behind.

Without trust and belief in yourself, it can be too easy to walk away before the environment around us has caught up (I previously mentioned this as Growth Jet Lag, which I'll get to in more detail in a later chapter). When you make changes in your life and business, there's an unknown period of time during which you may not see results of your actions. Trust that recognition will come. Trust that the world is catching up. Trust that the algorithm of life is doing its thing, sweeping up data, and will circle back around. Trust is the fuel that keeps you going.

It's important to trust when you are filled with self-doubt, when circumstances seem to be conspiring against you. It's important to trust when just as you thought you were getting somewhere, something or someone pulls the rug out from underneath you. All you can do is trust.

How will you build trust? Trust is like a reservoir. You need a daily habit of doing something to increase your trust. It's a personal choice. Perhaps prayer works best for you. Or meditation. Or being in nature where you can feel small in comparison to the bigness of the world around you. There has to be something bigger than you to trust in, right? Maybe it's a daily reminder of who you are or why you're here.

My client Crystal does the most beautiful work to help people find their purpose. She shares the story that when her father died, she found a journal in his nightstand; on one page, in large letters, was written, "Why am I here?" The rest of the page was blank. It broke her heart that as wonderful as her father was and although she knew why he was here, he didn't. She vowed to help others fill in their blank page, to help everyone know why they are here. Once you have a sense of purpose, you can trust that, come hell or high water, somehow, you can make it happen.

Perhaps trust comes from above or all around us, but when we're self-employed, nothing could be more grounding or what we need to learn in order to manage the uncontrollable. To ground yourself and bring you back to a place of trusting when you need it, have a phrase or two to recite in your head. It will fill up your reservoir of trust like water in a lake. That reservoir of trust will be there for you when you need it, which will likely be far more often than you might have imagined.

Having a reserve of trust will stabilize your reactions, keep you on track, and keep you going. There are many lessons and memes that circulate around social media about persistence, not giving up, and picking yourself up after a fall. It's all inspiring, for sure, but trusting in yourself, in the support of others, and in what you don't know is conspiring to work on your behalf will establish the steadiness and strength to create sustainable success.

Next, I'm going to share my favorite personal daily habit and the most effective way I know to create positive flow in your life and business.

12

Create a What's Going Right Journal

THERE ARE some habits that are so effective, they are worth repeating. That's the case with what I call a What's Going Right Journal, which took up an entire chapter in *LINGO*. So, if you've fully integrated the practice of a What's Going Right Journal into your daily habits and you're sticking with it, feel free to skip this chapter. But if you're not familiar with this life-changing daily habit or your commitment to the habit is anything less than stellar, then read on.

First, let me share where the idea came from. I have always loved the idea of a gratitude journal or some way of capturing gratitude. The problem was, I never stuck to a gratitude practice. While I'm sure there are many beneficial effects of a gratitude journal, for me, I was looking for something with more tangible results. Without evidence of tangible results, it's hard to stick to a habit. I would always fall off the gratitude wagon which made me feel bad, which I wasn't very grateful for.

Also, gratitude seems very broad. Heck, if I wake up in the morning, I'm pretty grateful. I'm definitely grateful for blue skies and sunshine in the morning. And my dog, Indie. What could I be more grateful for? Well, there are my kids, of course. And friends, good food to eat, my mom, my partner, living by the ocean, and on and on. There is plenty to be grateful for in life. In fact, I think it's pretty unlimited. Gratitude is a great perspective in life and undoubtedly can change your attitude. But the better your attitude about what there is to be grateful for, the broader and less actionable it becomes. What most of us need to keep going with a habit is to see tangible results. The What's Going Right Journal will provide them.

Create Tangible Results

Being a busy business owner, you want not only a good return on investment, but also a good return on time invested. I particularly like that the What's Going Right Journal is efficient and doesn't take long to do. If you can find just ten minutes a day for this daily habit, you can see actual results. Is it worth it to you? More importantly, what's the consequence if you don't? You are far more likely to continue to ride the roller coaster of the self-employed life. Do you want off, and to create sustainable success on a more consistent basis? This is the most effective daily habit I know.

The What's Going Right Journal is just what it sounds like: you write down what's going right in your life every day. When we focus on this, we tend to see what's going right even more. The What's Going Right Journal ticks all the boxes. It's efficient, it works with priming, it provides noticeable results, and it creates an inward flow of things going right.

It also works with the science of the brain to rewire our human tendency toward the negative. You know how you can hear nine compliments and one criticism, but the criticism is what you focus on? Or you'll worry about something long before you need to, latching on to what "could" happen? We humans seem to come preassembled for negativity. By journaling what's going right, you are rewiring your brain to see the positive instead of the negative.

The What's Going Right Journal taps into our spiritual sensibility. Whether it's faith, the universe, vibration, or energy you believe in, we know that you'll get more of what you focus on, and that you have the power to create and manifest what you seek. At the very least, you can only recognize what you already know. That's priming. By paying more attention to what's going right in your life, you are far more likely to recognize more of what's going right.

How It Works

I personally prefer this as a morning habit in conjunction with my whole morning routine. If doing this in the evening works for you, go for it! Just find a time you can stick to.

Here's my entire morning routine, two hours before I get ready for the day. First, I make a sixteen-ounce cup of masala chai tea, boiling my plant-based milk and adding loose chai spices and black tea, plus a little natural sweetener. I steep and strain the tea, and mug in hand, I read for an hour. Then I take my dog for about a forty-five-minute walk along the bay. I return home, feed my little buddy, and head off to my sacred space. There, in front of my small altar, handmade from columns of a demolished temple in India and adorned with special and meaningful things, I do a ten-minute guided meditation. At the end of the meditation, I journal in my What's Going Right Journal.

I believe it's important to start each day and journal entry with "What's going right is..." in order to get your brain

By journaling what's going right, you are rewiring your brain to see the positive instead of the negative.

———————

there—to be thinking and seeking what's going right. Then just list things that are going right in all aspects of your life. Granted, I'm a little partial to noticing what's going right in my business life, because that's usually where I'm seeking the most tangible results. For example:

1. What's going right is I got a new client.
2. What's going right is I received a great referral.
3. What's going right is I'm meeting all of these influential people.
4. What's going right is money is coming in!
5. What's going right is *I love* the work I'm doing.

You also want to acknowledge positive ways that you are changing and growing. Maybe you see yourself being braver; you're proud of yourself for attending a networking event. Perhaps you're noticing that you are more confident. Definitely notice what's going right inside yourself as well.

You also want to observe what's going right in other aspects of your life personally; for example, the good fortune you had coming across the perfect piece of furniture for your home, the sweet thing your lover said, the good news about a friend or family member.

There's no limit here as to what you notice that's going right! The more the merrier! You'll likely find that once you get started, the observations will start pouring out of you. Will it always be easy to get started? Will it always be easy to find things that are going right? Absolutely not! There are times in our lives when it is a downright struggle to find something that's going right. But you know what? There always is. No matter how small or seemingly insignificant, there's always something going right. Sometimes you might just have to dig a little deeper. The key is in getting started. When it's a challenging time, just think of one thing. Then maybe another will come to mind. There's no limit, but neither is there a minimum number of things going right. The goal is, you want to maintain your habit during the best of times and the worst of times.

Besides, you need it most during the most difficult times. It's when it's hardest to see anything going right that you break through the negativity, the very real pain you are experiencing. That's when you can begin to reverse it by seeing what's going right. And that's why this is so magical.

Why It Works

Your What's Going Right Journal will work because you begin to see more of what's going right, which can offset the influence of negativity. You're shifting the balance from paying more attention to what's wrong to focusing on what's going right. It builds on itself.

Your daily habit of writing in your What's Going Right Journal does not have to be part of any other practice or routine. It is also up to you to find the time of day that works best for you. I know many people for whom this is an evening practice, and they capture what went right that day. That actually makes a lot of sense. My evenings are not very predictable, so I stick with journaling as part of my morning routine. It also forces me to capture what's going right overall as opposed to on a specific day. But it is completely up to you to design the habit that works best for you.

Again, the most important thing is that you develop the habit for your What's Going Right Journal and stick with it. It won't create the sustainability you want if you don't bother when it's too hard to see anything going right. It won't help you long term if you set it aside when things are going great and you think you don't have the time. That's exactly the point: if you allow your daily habits to ebb and flow with the good times and bad, you are an active participant in creating the ups and downs.

If you can see what's going right in the best of times as well as the most challenging times, that's precisely how you create stability and sustainable success. Have you ever gone in for a prescription for an antibiotic and the doctor or pharmacist said, "Be sure you finish the entire dose, even if you start feeling better"? If you stop the treatment too soon, the bacterial infection can come back. And the What's Going Right Journal is like the good probiotic creating a healthy ecosystem inside you that maintains your peak performance and assures that you maintain your health.

I personally have not experienced anything that has brought more tangible results and a general sense of stability and hope. The goal is to create sustainable success for you. To help you ride the natural waves of business and life with a greater sense of ease. Ups and downs in business are to be expected. But if at every step you focus on what's going right, how could it not help you stay steady and consistent? The What's Going Right Journal is a very important step so that you maintain your forward momentum and don't feel like you're taking two steps forward and one step back. It will keep you gaining more of what's going right.

As much as we can rely on ourselves to keep us going and steady, we also need to continually grow and rely on others. That's what you'll gain next.

13

Expand Your Thinking

TO CREATE sustainable success, you need a habit of collecting wisdom, information, and knowledge. You need somewhere to go for inspiration, grounding, and your next strategic idea. You need a habit of depositing into this well of inspiration on a regular basis so that you can withdraw as needed without everything falling apart. You probably already know how often you will need to withdraw in order to stabilize yourself in the ever-changing world of self-employment.

Gather Advice

I love the exchange of wisdom and knowledge. To me, it's deeply steeped in our human nature to gain wisdom, knowledge, and inspiration from others and want to pass it on. It reminds me of ancient storytellers and the interdependence of us all. I can honestly say I hold hardly anything dearer and more important as the gathering of wisdom and the desire to share.

One of my favorite questions or conversation starters is to ask what the best piece of advice someone ever received is or a quote they live by or perhaps a favorite book they would recommend. Why don't you give it a try:

What's the best piece of advice you ever received and from whom did you receive it? How has that advice influenced your life? _____

_____

_____

Is there a quote that you live by or that has particular importance to you? _____

_____

_____

What is the one book you think everyone must read? _____

_____

_____

_____

Here are my answers:

Best piece of advice: "No one will ever care about your life as much as you do." My father told me this. It has helped me threefold. First, it's the basis of my motivation to get stuff done in my life. I don't wait around for others to solve my problems or be the change I want in the world. Second, I realized that if no one is going to care about my life as much as I do, then it's my responsibility to do something with my life and accept responsibility for my choices. Many times, I've been asked about my feelings on failure or to share a story about a failure in my life. I always have to explain that I don't see failure in a typical way. To fully take responsibility for your actions is to accept the outcome of them—what one may deem failure—whether or not things went the way you wanted. You don't place blame

To create sustainable
success, you need
a habit of collecting
**wisdom, information,
and knowledge**.

———————

on yourself or others—it's about acceptance of what you can and can't control, and being at peace with the outcome. Third, my father's advice enables me to be far more accepting of others than my perfectionist self would likely be. If no one cares about my life as much as I do, I can't hold others to the same standards as I have for myself, my work, or my life. It enables me to accept that others are doing the best they can. This has been particularly helpful for me as an employer. I hire great people, leave them alone to do their work, and trust they are doing their best. In the end, no one is ever going to care about my life as much as I do, so I cut them some slack.

Given the advice, it stands to reason that I am not going to care about someone else's life as much as they do. We are separate people taking care of our lives the best we can and hopefully caring, sharing, and supporting one another along the way.

Favorite quote: "Your level of success will rarely exceed your level of personal development." I've already shared this favorite quote, said by Jim Rohn, several times in this book, and I truly do live by it. I'm sharing that wisdom with you in the format of the Self-Employed Ecosystem. You have to develop yourself first to increase your ability to receive the success you desire, then apply effective business strategies and have good daily habits to sustain it.

The one book I think everyone should read: I read so many books (one to two a week), that it's almost impossible to narrow it down to one. When I'm a guest on podcasts and asked a similar question, I adapt my book suggestion to the audience. But if I had to pick one, sort of like the one book you'd bring to a deserted island, I'd have to go with *Man's Search for Meaning* by Viktor E. Frankl. It's a classic filled with so many life lessons, I wouldn't know where to start in telling someone about it. You should definitely read it, if you haven't. What I took away most from the book is that how we look at things is always our choice. No matter how dire the situation is, as was the case for Viktor as a prisoner in a Nazi concentration camp, we can search for meaning.

I like to think of wisdom, information, and knowledge as a reservoir, a space within ourselves that we are responsible for filling up. The cool thing is, it's an unlimited reservoir. What we can gain from others is of unlimited capacity. It is a reservoir we need to feed into on a regular basis. Unlike a literal reservoir, this one has unlimited capacity so that we can grow and expand—a reservoir that is available to us, full of riches, when we need to tap into it.

Let's look at some of the places you can go to gather more wisdom, information, support, and knowledge.

Add to Your Wisdom Folder

The first habit I suggest is creating what I call a Wisdom Folder. (For me, it's a folder in Google Drive. I prefer to do everything in the cloud so I can save the wisdom whenever it comes along, no matter where I am. It often seems that the best wisdom bombs come along when you least expect them.) In your Wisdom Folder, I suggest compiling quotes, sound bites, and bits of wisdom that are very short and concise. The purpose of the Wisdom Folder is to have a place to go when you need "a quick hit," when you are feeling derailed but don't have the time or energy to read a whole insightful page or even a paragraph. That's why my twice monthly newsletter has a very specific format. It's curated content, the best information that I believe will be most helpful to my community, laid out under LISTEN (top three podcasts to listen to), WATCH (a video to watch), READ (top three book suggestions), THINK (a quick bit of wisdom to get readers thinking), and DO (an action step to take). The benefit of short and to the point is that you are more likely to absorb the information if it's not a big deal. Your time is short, so giving up time is always a big deal.

Your Wisdom Folder will serve you well in the ups and downs of self-employment. Feeling discouraged? There's a quote for that. Need a quick pick-me-up? You saved a bit of advice a friend emailed to you. Dragging a bit on a Monday? There are inspiring memes in your Wisdom Folder. Of course, to tap into these resources, you have to build them up. Collect these wonderful bits of wisdom for a quick hit to get you out of a funk, and they will serve you very well to smooth out the bumps and keep you going.

Podcasts as a Resource

As an experienced podcast host, obviously I'm going to point out that podcasts are a great way to gain the benefit of wisdom and information from others. Seriously, with a million or so podcasts out there, there's something for everyone. Having access to this volume of information in the past would have been impossible. Not anymore. It's all available on the device of your choice. And it's free! Podcasts are an amazing resource to gain information on a particular topic as narrow or as broad as you'd like. You'll also find motivational podcasts to keep you going and soulful shows to bring you home. No matter what you're looking for or need, you'll find it in the wonderful world of podcasting. Take advantage of information you can gain from bestselling authors, well-known thought leaders, respected business leaders, and change-makers.

Books Are Magical

Books—what can I say? You're reading one, so obviously you see the value of books as repositories of wisdom you can add to your vault. But no one captures the magic of books better than Carl Sagan:

> *What an astonishing thing a book is. It's a flat object made from a tree with flexible parts on which are imprinted lots of funny dark squiggles. But one glance at it and you're inside the mind of another person, maybe somebody dead for thousands of years. Across the millennia, an author is speaking clearly and silently inside your head, directly to you. Writing is perhaps the greatest of human inventions, binding together people who never knew each other, citizens of distant epochs. Books break the shackles of time. A book is proof that humans are capable of working magic.*

Sure, maybe the creation of books has expanded to include ebooks and audio, but the idea of books to get inside someone's head remains the same. They have the ability to connect people, as I hope this book has also done. Reading this book, you have stepped from perhaps a far outer circle into a closer one on the journey of Hug Marketing.

No matter how contemporary a book may be, it still holds the magic of ancient wisdom, as the art itself will remain forever. To add to your opportunities to grow, learn, and collect wisdom and information, I highly suggest a habit of reading. As I mentioned earlier, it's part of my daily morning ritual to sit, usually outside on my terrace overlooking the ocean, with a cup of chai in hand and read for an hour. Except Sundays. I usually try my best to give my brain a break on Sundays.

**The biggest risk
is not in
what you build**. It is in not
supporting what
you build.

Join Trade Associations

Perhaps not a daily habit in execution, but a good habit nonetheless, is to belong to your trade associations, even if your career or business spans a few different trades. Through your trade associations, there are likely many educational opportunities, annual conferences, and such—great ways to gather wisdom, knowledge, and information. The goal of belonging to your trade association isn't about being like everyone else in your trade, but rather using membership as a resource for ideas. I like to suggest to my clients that they belong to their trade associations while maintaining a filter of discernment. Take in the good information and disregard what doesn't serve you. Because the last thing you want is to be like everyone else.

I also believe it's important to belong to your trade associations as a measure of support for your industry. If you don't respect and support your industry, how can you expect others to respect and support you? Support the cause for the greater good. Being a member of an association can in fact become a daily habit if you participate in association groups on social media or are active in the organization itself.

Don't overlook that being self-employed is a trade in itself. The National Association for the Self-Employed (NASE) in the United States is one example of an organization that offers a plethora of resources and services to help you grow your business and assist you. If you are American, I highly recommend becoming a member at NASE.org for support and information. They are very active in Washington, DC, on behalf of self-employed business owners in the United States, to pass legislation to make the lives of the self-employed easier. Support your trade associations and look for opportunities to learn, grow, and expand.

Surround Yourself with Support

As often as possible, I try to say to self-employed business owners, "You may be in business *for* yourself, but you are not in
business *by* yourself." We need each other. Loneliness and feelings of being alone in business are some of the most common
feelings expressed among the self-employed. Funny how you
can be surrounded by people in a hectic world but feel alone.
That's because no one can fully understand our world unless
they are in it. The devotion, care, long and irregular hours,
obsessive thinking. This is partly why the community and support of other self-employed people is so important.

Also important is support of our new level of achievement
so that we don't retreat. I see this firsthand every day. My
two-month Small Business Branding program helps business
owners set out in the world with clear direction and a brand
message that attracts their ideal customers. My Small Business
Consulting program teaches the Self-Employed Ecosystem
in detail and paves the way for unstoppable success. But this
newly created success needs support in order to be sustainable,
which is why I set up the Self-Employed Life Group, available
to already enrolled clients to find the encouragement they
need. Without support, it's just too simple to undo the work
that was done, to take two steps forward and one step back—or,
more than likely, to take two steps back and realize you haven't
gotten ahead at all.

Again, support is critical to sustainable success. As independently minded as you need to be to be self-employed, that
does not mean you have to go it alone. You have way too much
of your life invested, and have invested far too much time and
effort, perhaps even money, to not "prop up" what you've built.
The biggest risk is not in what you build. It is in not supporting
what you build. To not get the support you need from trained

professionals and a community of other self-employed business owners puts all the big stuff at risk.

Another famous Jim Rohn quote is, "You are the average of the five people you spend the most time with." Therefore, you want not only to be careful with whom you surround yourself, but also to make it a daily habit to connect with some measure of support every day. Or at least as often as possible. You might hire a coach. Obviously, I recommend that. Having a coach you trust who serves as your all-encompassing guide is superimportant. You're an idea gatherer, a sponge for information, and if you are surrounding yourself with support as you should, you will find direction on your path. Having a coach who gets the whole picture is like having your own North Star, someone to keep you on track, who might hold your vision better than you do. They can remind you of the greatness within you when you need it, as well as provide the exact strategies you need because they know your business so well.

You could have an accountability buddy. Or you could belong to a group of peers who are in your industry, or not. Personally, I think it's important to be part of both types of groups. Hanging around people in your industry is great for finding out what's working and not working for others in the same field. It's also satisfying because you share a lingo. But spending dedicated time with people from a variety of industries other than your own can also be eye-opening. It's wonderful for cross-innovation, taking an idea that works in one industry and applying in your own. It's also like having a focus group at your disposal because you can test to see how an idea is perceived by people outside your industry. An objective view can be very helpful. I belong to groups of fellow speakers, podcasters, coaches, and authors. And I belong to a group of people from an array of other industries. I also coach both types of groups. I have to say, though, there's something really exciting about a group of self-employed business owners from a range of industries. There's such a fresh energy and so much opportunity for innovative thinking.

The next daily habit is all about keeping you going. How to get more out of your day, more of what you're capable of, and therefore, more sustainable success!

14

Switch It Up

S O MUCH is expected of us as self-employed business owners. You know, the many hats you wear. If you're like
many small-business owners, you are the CEO, COO, CFO,
CMO, CTO. WTF, you might exclaim! Plus, you're maybe
the janitor, maintenance, designer, and party planner. Is it any
wonder we feel like we're all over the place and overwhelmed?

When I first moved to Miami from New York City, people
would often ask why I had moved to Miami in particular. That
was usually followed up with, "Was it the weather?" I would
respond by saying it wasn't the weather, per se, it was the
benefits of the weather. You see, New York City challenges you
to be bolder, think bigger, and perform at a very high standard.
For the many years I lived there, I loved that Big Apple energy
and mentality. But when I visited Miami for what was supposed
to be a three-month stint, I realized something very powerful:
that my current work required a different type of space.

My career trajectory over the previous several years had
changed from being primarily a photographer to becoming a
coach, consultant, and speaker. With all there is to love about
living in New York City, one thing I think almost everyone can

agree on is that it's not the most relaxing place. In one form or another, you feel like you're "always on." What I realized during those initial three months in Miami was that as my career had transitioned from the fulfilling creative work of being a photographer to assisting others as a coach and speaker, I had to take care of myself differently. In one form or another, my work role now was primarily in support of others. I wouldn't change that for anything, but I had to recognize that supporting others is draining. In order to give to others, you are taking something from yourself. Sort of like another reservoir. If that reservoir doesn't have the ability to refill, it runs the risk of being depleted. To create success in your business, you have to protect your capacity within to serve others.

What I found in Miami was that the environment was fulfilling. It is the right environment when you are in a profession of giving to and supporting others. Becoming aware of this is what inspired me to move to Miami. Sure, the sunny days help. But the real reason is, it's restorative and affords me more capacity to serve others. More capacity to serve others means more impact. More impact means a life well lived.

Create the Right Space

The habit we'll be talking about in this chapter is space switching. Of course, we're not necessarily talking about anything as significant as moving fourteen hundred miles to a city where you don't know anyone and don't speak the predominant language. Unless that's the change you need to make! What we are talking about is space switching throughout the day in your current work environment to make it more efficient and easier to manage your various roles, and will bring out your best. This daily habit creates sustainable success by supporting you to

To create success
in your business,
**you have to protect
your capacity within
to serve others**.

_____

produce at your highest level, thereby increasing the likelihood of continuous success.

This applies whether you work in an office, at home, or (ideally) in a combination of spaces. The goal is, as it was for me in moving to Miami, to let the environment you choose for various tasks do some of the work for you. It's about triggering your brain when you enter each new space for that task at hand. The new space is conducive to efficiency, which is important to you because there's never enough time. It's true to who you are, since you are already wearing many different hats. And it's invigorating because, let's be honest, we're not wired for sameness.

Since you started your own business, I suspect there's a fair amount of creativity to who you are—enough that you can create something from nothing, as you have done in developing and launching your business idea. So, there's a good chance you also chase a few squirrels or shiny objects. That's OK. I'm a proponent of chasing squirrels to leverage creativity, as long as they are going in the same direction. I don't know about you, but I'd rather walk down the street with someone who is pointing out the trees, flowers, and buildings than with someone singularly focused on the destination. Yet, I get it: the downside of being all over the place is lack of direction and efficiency. Space switching is sort of a happy compromise. It appeases our need for constant stimulation in a productive way.

It works like this. Create a distinct space for all of your different tasks, or at least for as many of them as possible. And don't worry. This does not require a lot of space. You might want a space for your creative work, a space for your logical work, a space for writing, a space for thinking, a space for collaborative work... a space for your different roles and tasks. Does this mean you have to have a massive amount of space? Not at all! It's great if you can move around, but if space is restricted, it can be about how you alter a single space to take on different meanings. What you're aiming to do is trigger mental cues: instead of moving to a different space altogether, the trigger to get in the zone for the next task could be something as simple as always fixing yourself a cup of wonderful-smelling tea before settling in to do some creative writing. Little ritualistic gestures like this or, say, lighting a certain candle every time you go to do a particular task, can shift the energy of the space and prepare you mentally.

Have you ever been to a WeWork or similar type of shared workspace? Make no mistake, a lot of psychology has gone into designing those collaborative workspaces. You'll find large shared desks that encourage building relationships; it's known, too, that being in the proximity of others can actually encourage you to focus. (I always feel like a bit of a slacker if everyone around me has their head down and is getting work done while my mind is wandering.) You'll find phone booths for when you need privacy for a call or to block out all external influences for a while. There are lounging areas for feet-up sort of work. Glass walled conference areas add to the productive vibe as well as private conference rooms. Of course, there's a cafe area so you can get a beverage and a snack, and interact with others. There's even psychology behind the open, curved staircases you'll find in every WeWork space. Centrally located, they are designed to encourage collaboration as you pass fellow space sharers. (They also serve as a bit of a fashion runway to see who's coming—or is that just me?)

Why not set up your workspace to afford yourself the same luxury of various spaces to help initiate the work you need to do?

Let me lead by example and share my working spaces with you.

Writing Space: This entire book was written sitting outside on the terrace overlooking the ocean. I know, sounds painful, right? It's the most inspiring space I could find to put my head in a certain zone for writing. All content creation is done here.

Coaching, Consulting, and Podcasting Space: This area has a stand-up desk and is for client video calls and podcasting. I prefer to stand when doing this work to keep my energy up, and since it's where I spend the majority of my day, it's healthier to stand. This space is in my office, with a branded background featuring podcast artwork on the wall, my books visible on a bookcase, and a touch of artwork and personal artifacts. It's a professional-looking space reinforced by what I do. To me and my clients, it signals getting down to business.

Admin Area: This desk area shares with my coaching and consulting space, except now I sit. See, I told you: you don't need a lot of space. Just "shift" the space. This is for more "officey" sorts of things, the stuff I find boring, like paying bills and administrative tasks. I do, however, enhance the small desk area with a pleasant-smelling candle to make the mundane a little more manageable.

Work-Alone Area: This is my favorite environment in which to work. I have a stand-up desk that is suction-cupped to a floor-to-ceiling window. It's bright, cheerful, and I feel like I'm working outside. Natural light can do wonders, and I highly recommend having as much natural light as possible in the space where you spend a lot of time. In this environment, I work on anything that doesn't involve client interaction, because it's not set up for video. It can be, but as it's in my living room, it's more of a private space. This is where I do emails, review websites, and complete all other solo work. I will often have music playing. Sometimes upbeat and sometimes Zen-inspiring spa music.

Shared Workspace: Of course, this is not an option for everyone, but some variation may be. Like many, I work at home alone—except for my loyal canine companion, Indie. To be sure I get enough human interaction, I enjoy working at a shared workspace one to two days a week. If such a place is not available to you, a coffee shop or hangout of some kind can be just as effective. Interestingly, podcast guest Donald Rattner, author of *My Creative Space: How to Design Your Home to Stimulate Ideas and Spark Innovation*, provided research that states that we are at our most proficient when the level of ambient noise is about seventy decibels, which is about the noise level of your average busy coffee shop or shared workspace. I concur! I find I am incredibly productive in a shared workspace where there is a certain amount of "white noise" created by the environment. It's also just stimulating to be around people. Feelings of loneliness are so common among the self-employed, particularly if you are a company of one. Occasionally switching to a shared space environment can be just what you need!

No matter how much or how little space you have, the goal is to trigger you to get in the zone of your next task as quickly as possible, to feel the energy of the space you've created that matches the energy you need for that task, be it creative, relaxed, professional, or highly focused. You want a space for each hat you wear. The key is in no longer seeing your space as static, but rather as flexible, adaptable, and contributing to your productivity.

Let's consider some of the energy triggers you can add to a space. If space is limited, you can also accomplish this by "resetting the table," if you will, without changing the space. But I do highly encourage you to get creative and find a way to actually switch spaces.

The View: What you're looking at can support or distract from the task at hand. If it's creative work that requires inspiration "from above," an open view or a window to glance out of can be very helpful. With focused work, that might be distracting.

Your Posture: Sitting, standing, or having your legs up can each connote a different feeling. I spend most of my day standing not only because it's healthier, but also because it keeps the energy up. Standing is also better for voice projection, so I stand while I record my podcast and do all my video calls. But there's most definitely work that is best suited to sitting and lounging with your feet up. Similarly, it's why ergonomic furniture, designed to reduce musculoskeletal problems and improve circulation, has become so popular; it's not only for the numerous health benefits but also for the ability to change position throughout the day. One position for too long is not good for your body or psyche.

Visuals That Inspire: What's in front of you can also matter to your performance and motivation. Perhaps you put an inspiring message on the desk where you pay your bills—a message to be resilient and keep going! On my admin task desk, I have a statue of Buddha with open palms to represent abundance, and a cast iron sculpture of two open hands that represent receiving. I don't know about you, but when I'm paying bills or invoicing, I want to be in receiving mode as much as possible. Photos of loved ones as well as mementos of your successes can remind you of what you're working so hard for. The lanyard from each speaking event where I've received a standing ovation hangs from a bookshelf in front of me to inspire me and remind me of my accomplishments.

The Impact of Color: Color is often connected with mood and emotion. Consider the color of your workspaces as well as the accent colors. Do they need to be vibrant to initiate creativity or soft to evoke concentration? Though there's much research in the area of color psychology and how certain colors can manipulate moods, I personally feel that the impact of color is an individual experience. One person's red that causes alarm can be another person's fond memory of a red barn in the country. What colors spark a feeling in you?

Scents Set a Mood: Another factor in creating your various workspaces is to consider what elements have the strongest effect on you. My mood is very influenced by scent. I've always joked that it's because I am rather blessed in the nasal capacity area. When I was a child, my grandmother would say to me, "Don't worry, you'll grow into your nose." But I love a good scent to evoke a mood. Did you know Miami has a patented scent? It's one of the best marketing strategies I've ever come across. The scent is called Hope and it's pumped into the air conditioning systems of most hotel and residential buildings. I noticed the same smell as I went from building to building when I was apartment shopping, so I did a little investigating. A local business called Doctor Aromas patented this distinguishable scent, which has been adopted by many of the hotels and residences. The idea is that the aroma embeds a memory of your visit to Miami, so that every time you smell it, you associate it with the tourist city. When I have guests visiting my home, I will sometimes buy them a small diffuser with the patented Miami scent to remind them of our time together. Think about the power of smell to prepare you for your time spent in a particular space. Or how scent can shift the mood of a space you use for more than one task. I often burn a candle with a soft, calming effect when I'm giving a virtual presentation. It calms me down and enables me to deliver a better presentation.

Space Proportion: As a photographer, it always amused me that while my clients lived in ginormous mansions, they and their families would always congregate in the smallest

Consider the proportions of the space to **support your work objectives**.

---

rooms to have their pictures taken. I also studied landscape design for three years at the New York Botanical Garden and learned about the power of expansion and constriction to influence moods. There's a reason artists are drawn to lofty, high-ceilinged spaces—the expansiveness increases creativity. You need a lofty space to initiate lofty ideas! But when we want to cozy up with our loved ones or to read or write, we often find a smaller room or nook more conducive. I believe that space proportions can have the largest subconscious influence on how you work. Often, when a space we're working in isn't helping, we don't know why. It just may not feel right. It's usually because of space proportion. I mean, who wants to curl up with a good book in a large marble-floored ballroom? So consider the proportions of the space to support your work objectives.

These are just some of the things to take into consideration when designing your various workspaces. Keep in mind, the goal is to support you and the work you are doing. The more you can support yourself and bring out your best work, the far more likely you will produce work that makes you in-demand and memorable, which then creates sustainable success.

Conclusion: Daily Habits

As I bring the Self-Employed Ecosystem to a close, I want to once again stress the importance that each part of your business be working well. If one part of the ecosystem is unhealthy, the entire ecosystem is off. This is what makes our experience as self-employed business owners unique. No one fully gets this until they experience it. All three areas of the ecosystem—Personal Development, Business Strategies, and Daily Habits—must be built and maintained for you to have a fully operating business and happy self-employed life.

An Ecosystem in Nature

An ecosystem in nature proves that as part of the Self-Employed Ecosystem, the habits I've outlined in this chapter do work. In nature there are five elements in an ecosystem:

1. Energy
2. Water
3. Nutrients
4. Living organisms
5. Oxygen

In a side-by-side comparison, you can see that the five daily habits you've learned in order to create sustainable success are similar to what exists in nature.

Daily Habit	Natural Element
Building trust	Energy
What's Going Right Journal	Water (flow)
Gaining wisdom and knowledge	Nutrients
Interconnectedness with others	Living organisms
Space switching	Oxygen (space)

If these five elements are what sustain a healthy and thriving ecosystem in nature that is ever-changing and growing, I'm confident these five daily habits will create sustainable success for you and your business, if you apply them. You must apply them.

Daily Habits Workbook

Rate yourself on a scale of 1 to 5 every week for each daily habit. If that's too overwhelming, you can also use the space to reflect on a weekly basis.

	Week of ___	Week of ___	Week of ___	Week of ___	Week of ___
Trust Mantra					
What's Going Right Journal					
Wisdom Folder					
Gain Knowledge					
Support Received					
Your Environment					

Weekly Insights
Considering my daily habits, what did I do really well on this week?
Which of my daily habits need more attention?

15

What's Next?

ANY YEARS AGO, I watched a documentary about
people all over the world who lived to be more than
one hundred years old. The filmmakers studied a variety of cultures, examining lifestyles, living conditions,
and diet, looking for common denominators, all in the quest
to discover the secret to being centenarians. I don't think they
came to the conclusion they were hoping for, but I think they
reached a conclusion far more important.

The common denominator the filmmakers came up with
across all of the variables was that the people over one hundred
years old all had an unusual ability to accept loss. Think about
it: you're going to experience a lot of loss if you live that long—
of loved ones, jobs, spouses, even children.

I interpreted loss to also include the ability to accept
change—an acceptance and willingness to let go of what used
to be instead of hanging on to it as a loss. Accepting change has
everything to do with being successful in business. We often
find what got us here won't get us where we want to go now. In
business, we realize over time that what used to work doesn't
work any longer. If in our mindset we hold on too tightly to the

way things used to be, we are not embracing what the future could be.

Some people claim that technology has made business less personal. But in many ways, technology offers the opportunity to be more personal than ever. Whether companies use technology to make their customers each feel like one *in* a million or one *of* a million is up to them, not the technology. Frustrated, some business owners will claim that "it used to be so easy." Perhaps. But it doesn't help to stay in that mindset if you want to continue to succeed—it is better to embrace the current business environment to move forward. Besides, it's probably "not easy" because of a misalignment with the current way of doing business. There are also claims that today's consumers or younger generations don't value x, y, and z—but could it be that some companies just don't understand what has value to these customer demographics?

Like an ecosystem in nature, business is an ever-changing environment. It has to be to remain healthy. Likewise, how we adapt to change is equally important. The following are observations about change, ways to help you be your best, and words of encouragement to keep you going.

A New Model for Success

To understand the new model for success, we must understand the old model. It worked in the past—it's what got us here. But it won't get you to where you want to go.

The old model for success was based almost entirely on hard work, hustle, and grit. You outworked your competition to get ahead, maybe even stepped over a few people along the way. It was about marketing *at* people, convincing them of your value, and perhaps at times being a little less than honest. But it got the job done, right? Think about the phrase, "The end justifies the means." How do you feel about that phrase today? Kind of negatively, right?

Today, the end does not justify the means. The "means," how we get there and how we conduct ourselves along the way, matters. As it should.

In the old model of business, we *built* a business. In the new model of success, we *create* a business. When we build something, we tend to use more force, more action. When we create, yes, we take action, but we also leave room to allow. We allow ourselves to be inspired. We allow ourselves room for the unexpected. And we allow ourselves to receive.

That's not to say the new model for success excludes hard work. Not at all. In the words of Harry S. Truman, "imperfect action beats perfect inaction every time." We have to take action to get anywhere. The difference with the new model for success is that in addition to effort and hard work, there is also working with the powers that each of us holds within ourselves: the power to set clear and specific intentions, and the ability to trust in ourselves as well as the world around us.

The new model for success includes your ability to be comfortable receiving. This should be easy, right? But most of us are terrible at receiving. Somebody compliments us, and instead of just receiving it, we brush it off. We might say, "Oh, it was nothing."

How about in business? Ever struggle with getting paid what you're worth? I've spoken to enough business owners to know that not getting paid what you're worth is a chronic problem. Maybe it's because you have a hard time *receiving* what you're worth. Not seeing your own value causes you to accept less than you're worth, which only diminishes your value (in your own eyes), and on and on. It's a vicious cycle.

You can do all the work, put in all the long hours, and apply every strategy, but if you don't allow yourself to receive what you're worth, you are literally blocking your own success.

If I were standing before you and said in a somewhat aggressive tone, "Oh, yeah, you're going to get what you deserve!" would you see that as a threat or a promise? I've asked this question many times, and most people say they would see it as a threat because I said it in an aggressive tone. But if I were face-to-face with you and said, "You're going to get what you deserve," and I meant everything you could ever dream of in your life, why shouldn't I say that with every bit of the same "aggressiveness"? It actually has nothing to do with how it's said—it has to do with assuming "get what you deserve" means something negative, that you don't deserve it all or you simply can't believe it. Again, we have a hard time receiving. So, I mean it, you are going to get what you deserve. Receive it!

The new model for success also includes the ability to acknowledge your successes. We can be so hard on ourselves that we don't take time to see what we do well. We also often overlook our incremental growth. In the self-employed life, we rarely get to where we want to go fast enough, and it can be so chaotic, we don't even notice how far we've come. We have to take note of our growth, even the small wins and baby steps. This acknowledgment becomes the positive fuel source to counterbalance the negative fuel source we so often run on. It's sort of like success breeding success. When we acknowledge our accomplishments, we are keeping the ball rolling. Sometimes that's all it takes.

The challenge is that running our own businesses can be full of rejection. The deals we don't get, the missed opportunities, and the efforts that don't pay off. The persistence and tenacity of someone pursuing a dream is nothing short of amazing. I admit that my not-so-guilty pleasure is watching competition shows like *The Voice*, *World of Dance*, and *The Great British Baking Show*. The pursuit of a dream is really something beautiful to behold and it moves me tremendously. Particularly for those in performance, whether it's singing, dancing, comedy, or professional speaking, there is significantly more rejection than acceptance.

"I just knew it was something I had to do, regardless of knowing it would be a lot of rejection," said Antuan Raimone, a universal swing performer for the musical *Hamilton*. "It was my passion." He explained:

> *[To keep myself going,] I have maintained a journal about every audition I've ever done over twenty years, by far the majority of which I didn't get. But whenever I would get discouraged, I would look at my journals and see the work I was putting in. I know I'm uniquely good at what I do. I have confidence in that. Seeing the amount of work and effort I was putting in reminded me that really it has nothing to do with me. It was just that I wasn't a fit for reasons that have nothing to do with me or that I even know about. And often, in hindsight, I realized it worked out for the best that I didn't get that role, because something better came along.*

Similarly, this is how we self-employed business owners need to look at rejection: we have to see that it rarely has anything to do with us, so that we can acknowledge what we do well and keep moving. Acknowledgment is essential to the persistence it takes to be successful.

The new model of success requires letting go of old ideas about business and customers. It's not "us and them." Customers are not to be targeted and thought of as a means to the end we desire. It is a collaborative effort of serving others and in turn serving our mission. Being in business is not a position of authority, but rather a privilege to serve and contribute to the greater good. Customers are far more sophisticated and attuned to how they feel about the businesses and brands they choose.

Who customers or clients do business with today is largely based on whether that business is aligned with their values and whether it contributes to the world they want to create. At a minimum, most people today won't do business with brands that oppose their values. I have a long list of companies I will not support because their company values don't reflect the world I want to see in the future.

The new model of success is based on empathy, relationships, and, yes, speaking the lingo of your ideal customers. In the new model of success, the success you see will be in direct relation to your personal development and the energy you put out into the world.

Midlife Self-Employed

"I'm not dead yet."

It was my first call with prospective coaching client Ted. He had recently left an agency he had cofounded fifteen years earlier. Tired of the day-to-day, he was looking for something more. He was inquiring about coaching because he was looking for his next venture. At fifty-five years old and with much accumulated wisdom, he didn't want a career or business that would run his life, but he wasn't ready to be done completely. "I don't know what the future looks like. It feels very open-ended and I'm OK with that," Ted explained. "Retirement is not an option. I intend to keep going. I'm not sure what's next. I just know I'm not dead yet."

I'm just a couple of years younger than Ted and found what he was saying completely relatable. While our career experiences were very different in that I had always been self-employed, the feeling of gained wisdom from experience did not in any way mean I was willing to be put out to pasture.

**The new model
of success is
based on empathy**, relationships,
and speaking the
lingo of your
ideal customers.

I'm not dead yet, either. In fact, in many ways, Ted and I shared the feeling that we were just getting started.

When Marissa reached out for coaching, she was already a successful consultant in the medtech industry. She came to me with a world-changing idea: she was starting a nonprofit to help women in third-world countries get the medical equipment they need to save lives. No small feat, to say the least. Marissa is one of the most determined individuals I've ever met, and shortly after beginning our work together, she founded HERHealthEQ, which provides medical equipment for equitable health care for women across the globe.

Natalie Siston, founder of Small Town Leadership and executive at a Fortune 100 company, seemed to have it all at work: a well-paying job doing work she loved, a fantastic team, and even a boss who supported her personal ambitions from day one. What could possibly motivate someone to leave the comforts of a corporate job and take on the risk of being self-employed? What makes us want to put ourselves on the line and subject ourselves to the hardships that are inevitable in creating something from nothing? Even with all of the bravery and inner strength I've had to find in myself over the years, I sometimes wonder if I'd have the courage to step out of a very comfortable situation for the unknown seas of self-employment. When Natalie inquired about coaching, I had to ask her what motivated her; what her rationale was for leaving the securities of what she had. Her response speaks to the reason many of us would make such a bold move. She said, "I was complete."

In other words, Natalie felt she had gone as far as she could. Probably not when it came to job opportunities and promotions, but there wasn't enough personal growth opportunity left for her. In order to feel like she was living up to her full potential, she would have to step out of her safe job and steady paycheck and see what she was really made of. And I'll tell you, she's made of a lot! I expect we'll be hearing big things from Natalie.

Whether what's next for you is becoming self-employed for the first time in midlife or trying something new, I believe there's a special kind of magic about being self-employed at this stage. I believe you have that little something extra to offer in the way of wisdom and experience. You are showing our world that bravery, boldness, and a sense of adventure are not reserved for the young.

In *The Soul of an Entrepreneur*, David Sax points out a huge myth: that entrepreneurship is for the young and ready-to-hustle. In fact, a 2020 report called "Age and High-Growth Entrepreneurship," published in the *American Economic Review*, revealed that the average age of the owner of the fastest-growing new companies was forty-five years old. Against commonly held beliefs, midlife entrepreneurs actually have the highest success rates of start-up businesses.

That's not to say that younger entrepreneurs won't change the world. In fact, I expect Gen Z-ers to be very eager to start their own businesses, if not full time, then as a side hustle. They are creative, independently minded, and fiscally responsible. But one thing is for sure. We midlifers know we are not ready to be put out to pasture.

Mary Tess Rooney, founder and president of True Stride, refers to this as investing in your Value Vault. During one of our calls, she explained, "Your Value Vault is a physical, mental, and emotional account of all your experiences—including your treasured successes, epic fails, and everything in between—that have made you, you. Yes, the good, the bad, and the ugly."

Of particular importance, I believe, is the idea that we gain value as we get older. Society often leads us to believe otherwise. Mary Tess continued, "The reality is, the older you are, the more value you have to offer. Unlike what people commonly believe, you don't lose value with age. On the contrary, you are constantly gaining value and you deserve to feel appreciated in ways that matter. This understanding is critical as you stride into self-employed life in midlife."

Chip Conley, business leader, author, and speaker, is a leading voice on aging with value. Chip made quite a name for himself in the business world as the CEO of Joie de Vivre Hospitality for twenty-four years, and as the author of *Peak*. In 2013, he became head of global hospitality and strategy for Airbnb. What was most significant about his role at Airbnb was the value that founder Brian Chesky saw in having a man of Chip's age and experience join a company of far younger team members. As Chip explained in an interview on my podcast, "We have an opportunity now for five generations in the workplace."

As a result of his time at Airbnb and lessons learned with a cross section of five generations in the workplace, Chip went on to author *Wisdom@Work: The Making of a Modern Elder*. In 2018, he founded Modern Elder Academy. In my opinion, Chip is the leading authority on midlife, bringing the respect, understanding, and opportunity to this stage of life that it deserves. As a guest on my podcast, he said: "As we live longer and life expectancy increases, it's not that we're old longer. It's that we are in midlife longer." Boom! And that's why there's so much opportunity for midlife entrepreneurs. Driven by knowing there isn't an unlimited amount of time but feeling they aren't dead yet, the midlife entrepreneur wants to create the success they crave and make the impact they desire, and sooner than later. With still a good number of years left, the midlife self-employed business owner is out to create a second life. Or perhaps a third.

Whether you are becoming self-employed for the first time in midlife or stepping further into something more meaningful after years of being self-employed, you are showing our world that bravery, boldness, and a sense of adventure are not reserved for the young.

Bring Out Your Best

"We all have closets to come out of."

It's the opening line of my TEDx Talk. It was intended to be a compelling opening, and later in the talk, I joke about how when I came out of the closet to my mother, she said, "Is it because you moved to New York City?" But what does it mean to really come out of the closet, and how is it we all have closets to come out of?

The closet I am referring to in this case is your current state. Whether that's terrific or not so great, there's a good chance there's more in you than what you are currently showing the world. Maybe it's the current state of your business or your personal development or the action you're taking. Doesn't matter, actually. It's where you're at right now. Everyone has closets to come out of, meaning there is always more in you: more you are capable of, more opportunities available, more growth possible, and more in yourself to be proud of. And this sets up the ultimate paradox of being self-employed.

When living the self-employed life, we most often look to ourselves for the solutions we need, to find the information that will help us grow and the motivation to keep going. We also need to take responsibility when something doesn't work out. This is why self-employment can be fraught with feelings of loneliness. The paradox is that in this life of self-employment, it actually takes other people to help us go beyond our current state. We need others to see more in us than we can see in ourselves at this point. We need support and a community of people who understand. We need a sense of belonging.

To create sustainable success, you have to realize how interconnected you are with the world around you, and that, often, people see more in you than you see in yourself. And you need to believe them.

Whether you refer to it as leveling up, expanding, creating more success, or coming out of the closet, what we're talking about is you stepping into the next level of your capacity. This is an essential element of sustainability as well as expansion.

An ecosystem in nature is full of organic matter that is ever-evolving and growing. So are you and your business. Anything without movement ultimately decays. Let's make sure we understand that sustainability does not mean maintaining the status quo. We are not looking to stay the same. There's always more in us and we need to continually nurture our growth. Come out of the closet once, and then again, and again.

However, rarely can we do this ourselves. We're limited by what we expect of ourselves, how far we think we can go, and what we think we deserve. The best way I know to come out of the proverbial closet is to listen to what other people see in us and stretch into the unknown. Maybe that's by challenging yourself. Perhaps it's by getting out of your rote habits and trying something new. It could be that you push yourself to a new level physically or get yourself out of your comfort zone. Likely, it's by listening to the positive things people have to say about you and the compliments you receive. One of the exercises I often give coaching clients is to make a list of all the compliments they've heard throughout their lives. I ask them to pay specific attention to the compliments they want to brush off as if they are no big deal. They are probably the biggest deal! What comes so easy to you is probably your natural gift. When people point it out to you by means of a compliment, what they are saying is, *this is who you are at your highest value.* Listen to it. Receive it.

The Up-It List

Here's a fun and effective exercise you can do with a small group of people to bring out more in yourself, reach new levels, and come out of whatever closet you're sitting in. It's called the Up-It List.

Gather a small group, maybe three to five people. (I've done this exercise in large group settings and just divided audiences into groups of between three and five.) Each person takes a turn stating a goal and allowing the rest of the group to create their Up-It List.

Let's call the first person to speak Person A. Person A states a goal: "This year I want to make $250,000." Each other person in the group has an opportunity to raise Person A's goal. For example, you might say, "I hear you, and you're going to make $250,000 with a month off for a vacation." The next person in the group might add, "I hear you, and you're going to make $250,000 with less stress than you feel now and be happier than you've ever been."

Do you see how this works? You are helping one another to "up" the stated goals. That's why it's called an Up-It List.

Take turns going around your group, giving each person an opportunity to state a goal and have it raised. Not only is it great to be the person whose goals are being upped, but it's also truly an honor to participate in someone else's growth. With that honor comes some responsibility to support one another properly. That's why there's a specific structure to the Up-It List exercise.

First, each response to the person's goal begins with, "I hear you, and..." We want to make sure they feel heard and acknowledged regarding where they're currently at and what they believe in for themselves. It's just that you can see more

In the new model
of success, the
success you see will
be in direct relation
to your personal
development and the
**energy you put out
into the world**.

---

in them, which is why you say, "and . . . ," then add to their goal. It's kind of like improv, in which one of the core tenets is "yes, and," which means you acknowledge and keep building.

The second important structure point is to reiterate their goal. Again, it lets them know they've been heard. It's also helpful to hear the goal again in direct comparison to the upped goal.

The third important structure point is the amount you increase their goal. It shouldn't be unrealistically crazy. If someone stated their goal was to make $250,000, don't come back with $1 million. It's such a big difference that it's easy to disregard. You want the look on their face to be, "Hmm, it's possible." It's also helpful to go beyond the obvious. Just because someone states a financial goal, doesn't mean more money is the best addition to their goal. That's why in this example we added a monthlong vacation, less stress, and being happier than they've ever been. If you know the person well, think about adding what you know they really value in life.

Let's look at another example, a real-life example involving my coaching client, Melissa. We played the Up-It List game in a small group via a Zoom video call. Melissa is a world traveler and is always flying somewhere.

She said, "My goal this year is to take a trip once a month." Someone upped her goal with, "I hear you, and see you taking a trip once a month and being upgraded to first class six of those times." You can't imagine the excitement in Melissa's voice when she contacted me to tell me that her very next flight was upgraded to first class! She knew she was on her way to living her Up-It List.

The Up-It List can be a great exercise to include periodically in a group to which you belong. In my Self-Employed Life Group, every now and then, we do the Up-It List, and it's always a lot of fun, and without a doubt, everyone leaves the call feeling uplifted and expanded. Who doesn't need that?

Growth Jet Lag

Growth Jet Lag is truly one of the most important things you can know about so you never give up on having the strategies in this book work for you.

As you are making all these changes to your mindset, applying all these business strategies, and incorporating the daily habits I presented, it will take a while for the world around you to catch up. Do not expect immediate change.

There are varying opinions on how long it takes for a change or habit to stick. Some say thirty days. Others say twelve to eighteen months. In my experience, it's somewhere in between. Here's the important thing. Lean in even further, because this is big. How quickly or long it takes for the world to catch up with the changes you've made is in direct proportion to your consistency and effort in all three elements. Consistency most of all. I like to think of it as reward and respect. If you consistently show up, putting in the effort to develop yourself, work on your business, and maintain your daily habits, respect and reward are shown in return. If you're a slacker (you won't be!) you can't expect the results you want any more than you can plant a weed seed and yell at it to become a flower.

So, effort, consistency, and patience. In my experience, with good, solid effort and consistency, you can see noticeable results in six to eight months of really enacting change.

Don't Give Up On Your Dream

"I'm backing out."

I called my cowriter for the TEDx event I was speaking at in just a month to tell her I couldn't do it. So much had gone wrong in a short period of time. Business, personal—you name it. Do you know that feeling, when you just can't go on? In this case, I felt I literally couldn't go onstage. I was tired of pushing through as a "professional," drained from always doing what was expected of me. Besides, I thought it would be inauthentic of me to give that TEDx Talk when my life wasn't all hunky-dory. The real truth was, I was about to deny myself a long-held dream because of what seemed like uncontrollable circumstances.

The irony was, my TEDx Talk was about expectations and how they keep us in a closet based on our limited views of ourselves. The only way "out of the closet" is to allow others to see more in us than we see in ourselves. How could I do that if I was hiding what was really going on for me? I was pretending everything was fine, when on the inside it wasn't. "Fake it till you make it" may have worked fine when I was in my twenties, but at this stage of midlife, it's all about truth and authenticity.

I was reminded of how often as self-employed business owners we push ourselves through sickness to fulfill an obligation or get the money to pay our bills. Or how often we brush aside our personal problems to come through for someone else. How often we suffer in silence, thinking we are the only ones going through something. We never are.

I was facing a dilemma: "Should I be true to my word or true to myself?" And at this moment, in February 2018, I decided to be true to myself. When I expressed my conflict to the cowriter, and editor of my book *LINGO*, Anjanette "AJ" Harper, she was not having it. "You've worked for this for years," AJ said. Two years of filling out TEDx applications and twelve prior rejections, to be exact.

"I know, AJ, but I just can't do it," I said. "I can't give a talk about expectations without feeling like I'm lying. So much unexpected has happened that I don't feel like I'm being authentic." I also knew that if you attempt to be anything less than authentic onstage, especially the TEDx stage, the audience will eat you alive.

This was Monday, so AJ requested that I give it until Thursday before I notified the organizers. Thursday came and AJ called to see how I was feeling. It was still a no for me. She begged that I give it the weekend to decide. I agreed.

One obligation I had that evening was to take my client Cece out to dinner. She had flown into Miami to work together one-on-one. Honor your obligations, right? I took Cece to one of my favorite spots and hottest neighborhoods. Wynwood is the art district of Miami, full of galleries and cafes, and internationally known for street art. We walked into one of the most well-known galleries in town, owned by and featuring the artwork of one of the world's preeminent pop artists, New York City–based Peter Tunney. And there it was, on the wall: a very large, spectacularly beautiful painting in the mixed-media collage for which Peter is known, saying:

"Expectations are the blueprint for disappointment."

Are you freaking kidding me? I think I looked around to see if I was on *Candid Camera* or if this was some weird social media experiment. I was supposed to be giving a TEDx Talk about expectations, which was turning out to be nothing like I expected, and here was this enormous painting staring me in the face with its uncannily relevant message.

I stepped up to the painting for a closer look. At $150,000, that incredible piece of art wouldn't be coming home with me. But I decided to ask the person behind the counter if there was a less expensive print available. It was a different guy than I'm used to seeing at the gallery, and I'm there pretty frequently.

"Excuse me, is there a print of that piece?" I asked, pointing to the wall on my right. As he stepped out from behind the counter, I noticed his jeans were covered in paint. I looked up from his pant legs and asked in a shocked tone, "Are you Peter Tunney?"

"Yes, I am."

"But you're never here. So glad to meet you," I said with an outstretched hand.

He reciprocated the handshake and brought me over to the print case. He slipped the print from the plastic covering. I glanced at the price. I hadn't intended to spend three thousand dollars on my way to dinner but felt I didn't really have a choice at this point. I mean, I was standing there with the artist. How could I back out now?

I explained to him the significance of the words he had created and all about my TEDx Talk. He listened intently, then slipped a pencil from behind his ear, asked my name, and signed the print. *Well, it's mine now,* I thought. He handed the print to me and said, "Here, my gift to you."

Stammering, I said, "You can't do that. I mean, it's super-generous, but I couldn't. You can't..."

"The hell I can't," he shot back. "It's my business and I can do whatever I want."

Then he leaned in. "You know," he said, "You think I'm giving you a gift. I'm here because I've had a shitty day, and your story about what this means to you and your TEDx Talk is exactly why I create art. You think I'm giving you a gift, but the truth is, you are a gift to me tonight."

With that, I ended up with the most beautiful piece of art, hand-signed with a personal message from the artist, that now hangs in my living room. It was a moment I will remember for the rest of my life. We exchanged handshakes and business cards, and Cece and I went off to dinner.

Of course, I did that TEDx Talk, which, much to my shock, was later added to the main TED website (TED.com). Can you imagine if I had backed out? If I had allowed what seemed like uncontrollable circumstances, the craziness of life, the realities of being self-employed, to control my decisions and my life?

Looking back, I can't believe how dangerously close I came to giving up on a dream, years of hard work, and all the opportunities that have since come along from that TEDx event, as well as the people I met and meaningful relationships I formed. I don't mind being vulnerable, and I always strive to be authentic.

That said, sharing this story makes me uncomfortable. I should have known better. After decades in business and considering myself so highly trained as a coach, how could I have come so close to giving up so much? That's how powerful the uncontrollable circumstances around us can feel when we are in business for ourselves. It's inevitable that what affects us personally is going to affect us in business, and vice versa.

The self-employed life has its challenges, but I'll bet you wouldn't have it any other way. You know you have a lot to offer and you do want control of your destiny. No matter what, don't give up on your dream.

Conclusion

A Beginning

A J HARPER, my good friend, publishing strategist, and editor of my book *LINGO*, gave me an interesting author exercise to do: I had to write the worst possible review I could think of for this book. Here's what I wrote:

This author has no right to write this book. It's full of concepts that are not fleshed out from unsubstantiated sources and by an author with no credentials in personal development! Let alone therapy! It pretends to be a business book, but really, it's nothing more than a bottom-shelf self-help book wrapped up in a lot of self-indulgent fluff. This author needs to spend some time on the couch if he hasn't already stopped sniffing the incense. Or drinking the Kool-Aid. There is simply no place in the world of business for sitting around the bonfire singing "Kumbaya." No substance. No purpose. Certainly, no reason to buy this book. I want to tell this author to get a grip, because he's going off the cliff real fast. Save your money. It's better spent on an enema.

I actually had way too much fun writing that! The point of the exercise was to face my greatest fear in writing the book, which is that readers might think it's too woo-woo for business and shouldn't be taken seriously, and that without a degree in psychology, I have no right offering the advice I am giving.

But here's the thing. I hold a very high value for walking my talk. The fact of the matter is, we self-employed business owners are scrappy. We have to be. We don't need business degrees. It's great if you have one, but you don't need one. We are in the business of figuring things out all the time. We solve problems on the spot; we pay close attention to what's going on and to those around us. We actively seek out opportunities and make judgment calls on the fly. I'm sorry, but no degree is going to teach you that. So, I walk my talk. If you're going to go out on a limb, as you do every day running your business, then I am going to go out on a limb and say what I feel needs to be said based on decades of figuring stuff out and observation from a place of curiosity, which began with selling eggs and continued with extensive training as a coach. Frankly, knowing that it takes getting pretty woo-woo to get money in your wallet, it would be irresponsible of me to hold back for fear of a bad review.

My hope is that *The Self-Employed Life* is the beginning of many good things:

- The beginning of us getting to know each other better

- The beginning of making changes to your business that bring you everything you could ever want in your professional and personal life

- The beginning of a movement of self-employed business owners getting the recognition for the impact we make on the world and economies

- The beginning of fair representation in governments that grant us the security and benefits we deserve

* The beginning of embracing the term "self-employed" with pride

* The beginning of my role not only supporting self-employed business owners to build the business and life of their dreams, but also being their advocate

* The beginning of your self-employed life where you really do control your destiny

I have to admit, I quivered a bit each time I wrote the word "control" in this book—for some, the word has negative connotations. Or maybe it's just me, because of all the times I was accused of being controlling in my life. But if my father was right in believing that no one is going to care about your life as much as you do, then who else is going to take control of your life? Why shouldn't you have control over your own destiny?

As I sit out on my terrace, watching the sun rise over the ocean, I'm reminded that every business decision I've ever made was first a decision about how I wanted to live. If that's being controlling, then so be it. I'm OK with that, and you should be too.

You deserve to have control over your destiny to the best of your ability in the uncertain circumstances of self-employment. And there are many uncertainties, every day, all the time. I'm confident that if you embrace the concept of your self-employed life being an ecosystem; take action on the business and personal development strategies I've shared here; fight back against the inclination to compartmentalize your life; stop listening to a traditional-thinking world telling you to focus on one thing; and know that it's OK to take it all personally because it is personal, you will control your destiny. You deserve that.

I truly believe the Self-Employed Ecosystem is the formula for your self-employed success. I believe that creating the environment for what you want to happen and trusting that it will come to be is the answer to almost everything in life.

Thank you for being you. For being awesome. For being brave and for representing self-employed business owners worldwide.

Here's to new beginnings. Here's to your self-employed life.

Acknowledgments

> *"A good writer possesses not only his own spirit*
> *but also the spirit of his friends."*
> **FRIEDRICH NIETZSCHE**

WHILE A book may be written in solitude, one is never alone when the spirit of so many friends and loved ones surrounds you while writing.

To my three kids, Connor, Clare, and Lilly: First of all, I don't have a favorite. Well, maybe on some days. But you are each my favorite in your own way because you are individually remarkable humans, and I am honored to be your dad and grateful for your friendship. I know every parent thinks so, but really, I do have the best kids.

Thank you, AJ Harper, for your deep, unconditional love and support. Maybe someday I'll figure out what I did right to deserve your friendship.

To Rob, my partner in this journey of life, love, and kayaking, thank you for your incredible support. Sometimes, I'm not sure if you really care about what I write, but your care for me always comes through in abundance. And you're so patient. I couldn't ask for more. Just stop looking twenty years younger than you are, because you're making me look old.

To the team at Page Two, thank you: Trena, whose support inspired me greatly to move forward with this idea; Amanda, my oh-so-patient editor and occasional therapist; Peter, the amazing designer of the most beautiful book cover ever; Chris, whose official role was marketing strategist but felt more like No. 1 fan; Gabi, the super-calm and steady force you need when everything is swirling; and Steph, for making sense of my words and creating a clearer message.

Thank you to my friends. There are too many to mention, but a special shout-out goes to Brant Menswar, Denise Jacobs, Mary Tess Rooney, and Roger and Nancy Pelissier.

I want to thank my podcast team, Enid, Colin, Cate, and Cheryl, for making me look and sound good. Also, Tom and Karen Schwab and the entire team at Interview Valet for getting me booked on podcasts.

I also want to extend my deepest gratitude to our Waffle Sunday crew. You know who you are. What you may not know is how much you enrich my life, bring me joy, and make Miami home when you show up to share a waffle or two and a mimosa (or several).

Lastly, I want to thank you, the reader, as well as all the podcast listeners and those out there yet to be connected with: thank you for trusting me, and for going on the Hug Marketing journey. Be your best self. Be proud. And keep changing the world.

Recommended Resources

I'VE MENTIONED numerous publications and podcasts in this book and collected them here for your interest. I highly recommend all of them!

Books

Chip Conley, *Peak: How Great Companies Get Their Mojo from Maslow* (Hoboken, NJ: Jossey-Bass, 2017).

———, *Wisdom@Work: The Making of a Modern Elder* (New York, NY: Currency, 2018).

Viktor E. Frankl, *Man's Search for Meaning* (Boston, MA: Beacon Press, 2006).

Michael E. Gerber, *The E-Myth Revisited: Why Most Small Businesses Don't Work and What to Do About It*, rev. ed. (Manhattan, NY: Harper Business, 2004).

Todd Henry, *Louder Than Words: Harness the Power of Your Authentic Voice* (New York, NY: Penguin Publishing Group, 2015).

Lynne McTaggart, *The Intention Experiment: Using Your Thoughts to Change Your Life and the World* (New York, NY: Atria Books, 2008).

Brant Menswar, *Black Sheep: Unleash the Extraordinary, Awe-Inspiring, Undiscovered You* (Vancouver, BC: Page Two, 2020).

Jamie Mustard, *The Iconist: The Art and Science of Standing Out* (Dallas, TX: BenBella Books, 2019).

Norman Vincent Peale, *The Power of Positive Thinking*, reprint ed. (New York, NY: Touchstone, 2003).

David Priemer, *Sell the Way You Buy: A Modern Approach to Sales That Actually Works (Even On You!)* (Vancouver, BC: Page Two, 2020).

Donald M. Rattner, *My Creative Space: How to Design Your Home to Stimulate Ideas and Spark Innovation* (New York, NY: Skyhorse, 2019).

David Sax, *The Soul of an Entrepreneur: Work and Life Beyond the Startup Myth* (New York, NY: PublicAffairs, 2020).

Jeffrey Shaw, *LINGO: Discover Your Ideal Customer's Secret Language and Make Your Business Irresistible* (Creative Warriors Press, 2018).

Rory Vaden, *Procrastinate on Purpose: 5 Permissions to Multiply Your Time* (New York, NY: TarcherPerigee, 2015).

Podcast Episodes

"Beyond the E-Myth: Go Big, Go Bigger!" interview with Michael E. Gerber, February 1, 2017, in *Creative Warriors*, podcast, 41:35, creativewarriorsunite.com/beyond-the-e-myth-go-big-go-bigger/.

"Making of a Modern Elder," interview with Chip Conley, July 31, 2019, in *Creative Warriors*, podcast, 45:51, creativewarriorsunite.com/making-of-a-modern-elder/.

"Self-Employed: Present and Future," interview with Keith Hall, May 6, 2020, in *Creative Warriors*, podcast, 41:18, creativewarriors unite.com/self-employed-present-and-future/.

"The Self-Employed Life Stories with Antuan Raimone," *Jeffrey Shaw: Being Self-Employed,* June 9, 2020, YouTube video, 20:45, youtu. be/kwxHJt78GYY.

"The Self-Employed Life Stories with Katie Vlietstra," *Jeffrey Shaw: Being Self-Employed*, May 26, 2020, YouTube video, 36:43, youtu. be/t9A7LQ_YPYQ.

Article

Pierre Azoulay, Benjamin F. Jones, J. Daniel Kim, and Javier Miranda, "Age and High-Growth Entrepreneurship," *American Economic Review: Insights* 2, no. 1 (March 2020): 65–82, doi.org/10.1257/ aeri.20180582.

About the Author

HOW MANY people can say they've never worked for anyone else? Selling eggs door-to-door at fourteen years of age began a lifetime of self-employment for Jeffrey Shaw. Now, as an experienced speaker and small-business consultant, Jeffrey helps self-employed and small-business owners gain control of their business in what otherwise seem like uncontrollable circumstances.

Drawing on his expertise as a renowned portrait photographer, Jeffrey shows business owners how to view their work through a different lens, and offers proven strategies for arranging the often chaotic pieces of life and business into a composition of sustainable success. Jeffrey's portraits have appeared on *Oprah* and CBS News, in *People* magazine and *O, The Oprah Magazine*, and are displayed at other prestigious locations such as The Norman Vincent Peale Center and Harvard University.

Jeffrey's TEDxLincolnSquare Talk, "The Validation Paradox: Finding Your Best Through Others," is featured on TED.com. He's the host of the top-rated podcast *The Self-Employed Life* and the author of *LINGO: Discover Your Ideal Customer's Secret Language and Make Your Business Irresistible*.

Jeffrey has three adult kids, and when he's not traveling, he's often hosting Waffle Sundays at his home in Miami, where friends old and new gather for homemade waffles, a mimosa or two, camaraderie, and genuine connection.

jeffreyshaw.com
theselfemployedlife.me

Want Jeffrey to keynote
your next live or virtual event?

Credit: John DeMato

Get in touch with Jeffrey Shaw's
speaking coordinator at *speaking@jeffreyshaw.com*
or book Jeffrey at *jeffreyshaw.com/speaking*

**An in-demand speaker for
association conferences and events!**